Exploring what we won't find (or miss!)
in Heaven or on the New Earth

RAINBOW
CITY

ROBERT E. DRAKE

Copyright 2021 by Robert E. Drake
rainbowcity.feedback@gmail.com

All rights reserved. No portion of this book may be reproduced, stored in a retrieval system, or transmitted in any form or by any means—electronic, mechanical, photocopy, recording, scanning, or other—except for brief quotations for review or citing purposes, without the prior written permission of the author.

Unless otherwise noted, all Scriptures are from the New King James Version®, copyright © 1988, Thomas Nelson, Inc., Publishers. Used by permission.
Scripture quotations with the notation KJV are from the King James Version of the Bible.
Scripture quotations with the notation NLT are taken from the Holy Bible, New Living Translation, copyright © 1996. Used by permission of Tyndale House Publishers, Inc. Wheaton, Illinois 60189. All rights reserved.

Published by Argyle Fox Publishing
argylefoxpublishing.com

Publisher holds no responsibility for content of this work. Content is the sole responsibility of the author.

ISBN 978-1-953259-19-6 (Paperback)
ISBN 978-1-953259-20-2 (Ebook)

Table of Contents

PART I: Introduction

    Welcome to Rainbow City!..1

    Spark Your Imagination!..3

PART II: Our House

    The Bathroom..7

    The Bedroom..11

    The Clothes Closet...15

    The Laundry Room..17

    The Living Room..21

    The Kitchen..28

    The Dining Room..31

    The Office..33

    The Garage..38

PART III: Our Community

    The Neighborhood..45

    The City..50

PART IV: Our Attitudes

    Fitting In with the Family of God....................................59

PART V: Myths about Heaven

    Myth #1: Halos, Clouds, Harps, and Wings..................71

    Myth #2: Singing, Singing, and MORE Singing!........74

Myth #3: Fire Insurance—a HOT Topic!...................75

Myth #4: A Topic of Concern to All—Oh NO!......78

Myth #5: BIG Oops—God Made a Mistake!............83

Myth #6: No Physical Bodies...86

PART VI: Troubling Answer to a Trick Question

What Jesus Said and Why..89

What Jesus Didn't Say and Why.....................................98

PART VII: The Most Important Thing in This Book

Trust in the Lord with All Your Heart........................105

PART VIII: Final Thoughts

Epilogue...111

Author's Postscript..117

About the Author..121

Dedication

†

To my father,
Arch Louis Drake
1909–2003

†

When I was just a young boy, my dad's vivid description of dreams God gave him in the night about Heaven and the New Earth inspired a life-long fascination for me about these subjects.

Since then, I have developed a firm belief that the great battle between Good and evil is rapidly coming to an earth-shattering milestone, marked by the second coming of Christ. But no matter how far into the future this event occurs, the Bible says it could also seem to happen just a split-second after our last breath.[1]

Therefore, I'd like to further dedicate this book to all those who, by the grace of God and their own personal experiences, have developed a deep longing for a better place.[2] My prayer is that this book would inspire a more meaningful vision of the places Holy Scripture describes as Heaven and the New Earth.[3] Amen!

---

[1] 1 Corinthians 15:51–52
[2] Hebrews 11:13–16
[3] Revelation 21:1

PART I
INTRODUCTION

Welcome to Rainbow City!

Have you ever wondered what it will feel like to live in Heaven? Living eternally means there will be absolutely NO time limits on the living, learning, and loving you and I, alongside the saved of all generations, can experience and enjoy. Praise God forevermore!

The Apostle Paul gives us our first clue about Heaven by stating, "No eye has seen, no ear has heard, and no mind has imagined what God has prepared for those who love him."[1] In other words, it is beyond our present ability to fully understand what we will experience and enjoy in Heaven. However, a careful study of the Holy Scriptures will reveal enough information about Heaven for us to use the gift of our *deductive*[2] reasoning skills to *infer*[3] a surprising number of things which we most likely won't find (*or miss!*) there.

---

[1] 1 Corinthians 2:9 NLT

[2] Deductive—The process of reasoning from a premise to a logical conclusion.

[3] Infer—The process of weighing all available evidence to derive a logical hypothesis or opinion based on facts known, or rationally assumed, to be true.

Taking this approach gives us an opportunity to employ the same compare-and-contrast method Jesus used so effectively in many of His parables to illustrate important concepts and principles. I believe this same method can still be used with today's young people and adults who have lost a spouse to effectively counter many of the false concepts and troubling distortions our modern culture and media have promoted about Heaven and the New Earth.

But with that said, it is also **very important** to avoid making the Scripture-based deductions and inferences in this book into unfounded speculation and fantasy. When in doubt, always err on the side of the plainest biblical teachings.

Remember, God's original purpose for the human family was for us to live eternally as a happy, healthy, holy people whose natural response would be to praise our Creator and to enjoy each other.[4] Had Adam and Eve not fallen, it would have been our privilege to live forever free in joyful harmony with all the unfallen beings in God's vast and magnificent universe. Thank God that, in the near future, His original purpose for mankind will no longer be denied![5]

---

[4] Isaiah 65:17–25 NLT
[5] Acts 3:20–21 NLT

Spark Your Imagination!

To begin, I would like to spark your imagination by using a common, down-to-earth, illustration—a modern family home. We will explore my own family home room by room and discuss what we find. Then, we will think about whether or not it really makes any sense to want or need the same things in our heavenly home.

When we are done with our house, we will take a drive around our community. Again, we will follow the same scenario of carefully considering if what we experience with our various senses would be wanted or needed in Heaven or on the New Earth.

Next, we will explore some of the attitudes we humans have to put up with on our present earth. There are numerous comparisons of attitudes in the Bible which we must consider in the context of fitting in and living eternally with the family of God in Heaven.

We will also exercise our *deductive* and *inferential* reasoning skills to address some common myths about Heaven. And we'll carefully consider several possible perspectives on questions about human relationships there which have historically bothered both young and old alike.

Finally, I'll share how important it is to trust the Lord with our past, present, and future, both on earth and in Heaven, **especially** concerning the things we don't understand.

But, before we begin this journey, I would like to reassure you on one very important point. Even though our *deductive* and *inferential* reasoning process may seem to rule out many things which are commonly found in our daily lives in the here and now, no one will actually miss anything that is truly beneficial.

You may legitimately ask how we can be sure of this. The answer is simple—we serve a God who is omnipotent in creativity, omnipresent in power, and omniscient in His love for you and me. This, my friend, is absolutely the best guarantee you and I will ever have for our eternal happiness and complete satisfaction.

PART II
OUR HOUSE

Welcome to our house! We like to make our guests feel as comfortable as possible. Since Jesus stated that He was "going to prepare a place for us in Heaven,"[1] then it would seem logical to start our *deductive* and *inferential* reasoning processes by making some comparisons between what we find in our homes right now and what we might (or might not!) find in our homes there.

So, let's start with . . .

---

[1] John 14:2 KJV

The Bathroom

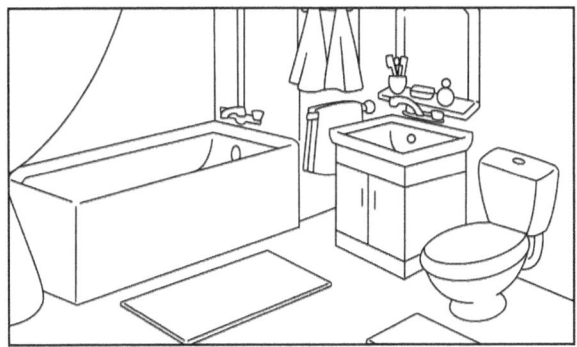

Whenever a teacher of elementary-age kids opens the floor to questions about Heaven, one that often emerges is this: *"Will we have to use the bathroom there?"* To be honest, the Bible does not mention toilets, urinals, or outhouses in Heaven. However, it does mention that nothing which is unclean, defiles, or decays will be there.[1] This description would certainly seem to include human waste products of all kinds.

We also know our human bodies will be completely transformed during the resurrection and/or translation process. Holy Scripture repeatedly states the saved shall be changed into the same kind of perfectly designed, radiantly healthy, human bodies that God originally made for Adam and Eve to enjoy.[2] So, with a perfectly functioning body, it would be hard to imagine any waste materials being left over from eating perfectly nutritious food, drinking perfectly pure water, and breathing perfectly pure air.

To employ our *deductive* reasoning process a bit further, I would also have a hard time imagining a sewer system in the New Jerusalem or septic tanks buried behind our country homes. Nor could I picture

---

[1] Revelation 21:27
[2] 1 Corinthians 15:51–52 KJV, Philippians 3:21 KJV, Zechariah 9:16–17, Revelation 21:4 KJV

wastewater and sewage treatment plants cluttering the landscape. And I'm absolutely certain there will be no drainpipes emptying pollution of any kind into the River of Life.

Let's think about another aspect of this topic. Since the Bible indicates that all the animals God originally designed and created for the Garden of Eden will be there,[3] my guess is that they will have perfectly functioning bodies too. I can't imagine the alternative of having to carefully step around odor-producing piles of manure in the otherwise beautiful meadows, magnificent forests, and majestic mountains of God.

I may be going out on a limb here, but I believe it would be safe to assume we will not need any type of toilet or urinal fixtures in our heavenly homes. Nor do I believe the animals will be leaving behind a trail of unsightly waste products. No pooper scoopers or litter boxes needed!

As we look around the bathroom in my house, we notice a medicine cabinet. Now this is an easy question to deal with, because the Bible is very clear about no one getting sick, injured, disabled, or having allergies, muscle aches, or headaches of any kind in heaven.[4] Thus, no need for medicines, bandages, thermometers, or disinfectants. Yay!

Now, let's consider the bathtub, which is the fixture the bathroom is named after. This was a hard one for me because, quite frankly, I love our bathtub and shower. And I truly think the modern hot water heater is one of mankind's greatest inventions. But aside from the pleasure of soaking in warm water, what are the real reasons we take a bath or shower?

Unfortunately, since sin has entered the world, the Bible says man must earn a living by the sweat of his brow.[5] And as everyone knows

---

[3] Acts 3:20–21 KJV
[4] Isaiah 35:5–6 KJV, Revelation 21:4 KJV
[5] Genesis 3:19 KJV

from personal experience, when we sweat, we don't *smell* so good. When our skin feels hot, sticky, and dirty, we also don't *feel* good. The most immediate solution is to take a bath or shower with some soap and lots of clean water.

Why does the soap work? Well, the short answer is that the combination of soap and water helps to lift and remove the layer of sweat, dirt, and bacteria from our skin, which causes us to smell bad and feel sticky. But what if we *never* had this problem to begin with because our perfect body could regulate body temperature without breaking a sweat, no matter how hard we work or play?

And what if the atmospheric temperature, humidity, and pressure were so perfectly balanced that we could enjoy that clean, fresh, just-bathed feeling all the time? Would we still need a bathtub or shower, soap, shampoo, and conditioner? I don't think so.

But lest you fellow water lovers fear you'll be missing out on something in Heaven, let me remind you the Bible says there will be plenty of completely clear, clean, fresh water available. Does the River of Life and the Crystal Sea ring any bells?[6] And what about all the beautiful waterfalls and the geothermal hot springs that are so prized in many countries here on our present earth? God is the original inventor of the shower and the hot tub!

So, there is certainly no reason why we couldn't have some good, old-fashioned, *clean* fun in the water. Instead of a bathtub, how about a natural hot spring to soak in with your loved ones, situated right on the ground floor of your heavenly mansion? And instead of a shower, how about a waterfall of warm, crystal-clear water to enjoy, flowing right through different levels in your country home? And instead of a bathroom sink, how about a real fountain gently bubbling up fresh, cool, delicious water right in your own home? No artificial plumbing, faucets, or drainpipes needed.

---

[6] Revelation 22:1 KJV

Near our bathroom sink, we keep a variety of other items, such as shavers, nail clippers, toothpaste and toothbrush, mouthwash, and hand soap. I honestly don't know if we will need periodic haircuts, shaves, and manicures in Heaven. God might genetically engineer our immortal bodies to grow just the right length of hair and nails, and then stop growing. Who knows for sure?

However, I *do* think it is safe to say we will not have any tooth decay or bad breath, which are both caused by bad bacteria. So, there will be no need for a toothbrush, toothpaste, or mouth wash. Nor will we have dirty hands needing to be washed before every meal. I'm just not sure what we will use a bathroom sink for in Heaven, but it will be great to see if our heavenly mansions are equipped with one.

Now, let's move on to . . .

The Bedroom

The bed is a piece of furniture which the bedroom is named after. However, I'm not sure we'll actually need a bed in Heaven. Why, you ask? Well, for starters, we will never feel tired or irritable from overwork or aggravation.[1] We will never have a headache from studying too hard, a body ache from playing too hard, or a hangover from staying up too late.[2]

So, what must it be like to be forever free from any type of physical, mental, or emotional fatigue? We simply can't imagine it because sleeping is something every human being naturally craves at least once (and for some of us, more than once!) every day of our life, from the day we are born until the day we die.

However, the Bible does mention that even God the Father *rested* from His labors during Creation week.[3] Does this mean creating our little world somehow wore Him out, or that He needed to go horizontal for a while to recover from His labors? No. I think the word *rest* as used here simply means that He stepped back for a day to admire and enjoy the results of His handiwork.

So, what will we use a bed for in Heaven? I don't know. But Heaven

---

[1] Isaiah 35:10 KJV
[2] Isaiah 40:31 KJV
[3] Genesis 2:1–3 KJV

surely won't involve spending one-third of our time in an unconscious state so our body can repair itself from the damage of being awake and active during the other two-thirds of our life.

Since we have a winter season where we live, you will find a very nice electric blanket on our bed. But will we need one in Heaven or on the New Earth? I think not. A perfect climate automatically comes with a perfect temperature and humidity level. Therefore, no need for blankets or a central heating system to keep us warm and comfortable in our heavenly mansion.

What about my beloved electric fan, which has faithfully circulated the air in my bedroom every single night for the last fifty years? Again, a perfect climate would include gentle breezes of the most delightfully fresh, invigorating air you can possibly imagine. No need for a fan, air-conditioning, or house insulation of any kind.

There probably won't be any screens or glass in the windows either. Think about it. A perfect climate means no storms. Perfect animals mean nothing dangerous or bothersome, including flies or insects to keep out. And perfect human beings mean no criminals to worry about. So why would anyone need screens and glass in a window or doors to close and lock? We will feel (and actually *be*!) perfectly safe and secure at all times, everywhere in God's great universe.

Now, let's talk about my alarm clock. This is a device used for waking up from an unconscious state of sleep at a predetermined time. This is usually so we won't be late for an appointment, such as for work or school.

So, what kind of appointments would one have up in Heaven or on the New Earth? The Bible does mention Sabbath worship, so that implies our current seven-day weekly cycle will continue both in Heaven and on the New Earth.[4] The sun and moon are also mentioned as still existing at that time, with both providing considerably more light than they currently do.[5]

---

[4] Isaiah 66:23 KJV
[5] Isaiah 30:26 KJV

The Bible says there will be no nighttime *inside* the New Jerusalem, due to constant light from the glory of God.[6] But, assuming the New Earth continues to spin one complete revolution every twenty-four hours, there will probably be some form of naturally increasing and decreasing light *outside* the city walls from the sun and moon as they mark off each of the seven days in our weekly cycle.

But wait a minute! (Oops, there we go again with one of our many idiomatic expressions for time.) Doesn't the Bible say, "time shall be no more"?[7] Actually, this verse is not referring to timekeeping in Heaven at all. The angel is talking about no more delay in the second coming of our Lord and Savior Jesus Christ. But there are many other verses in the Bible which paint a picture of the saved being forever free from the *negative effects* of time as we know it.

So, what are the *negative effects* of time? As people get older on this present earth, their reflexes slow down, fine motor coordination deteriorates, joints begin to ache, and muscles lose their tone. To make matters worse, eyesight and hearing often begin to fail, and some people even lose their mental abilities. Beyond all that, the stress of having more to do than we can get done each day wears most of us out and causes us to lose sleep and suffer fatigue and a variety of other ailments.

When we were children, it seemed like we couldn't get older fast enough. But when we eventually became older, then it seemed like we couldn't stay young long enough! In Heaven, we will grow up to and remain at the very peak of physical, mental, and emotional development, just like God originally intended for Adam and Eve.[8]

But back to the question of an alarm clock. If we never have a physical or mental reason to sleep, then why would we need some device to wake us up? I'm not going to go so far as to say we will never want to take an old-fashioned nap. But if we do, I'd like something else to wake me up besides the noise or artificial music of an alarm clock.

---

[6] Revelation 21:23–25 KJV
[7] Revelation 10:6 KJV
[8] Acts 3:21 KJV

14 / OUR HOUSE

The most pleasant "alarm clock" I have ever experienced was gently waking up at sunrise in a grass-roofed hut near the beach on a southern Philippine island. The air was filled with the sweet, soft warbling of dozens of tiny birds singing their hearts out on the roof and in the branches of nearby trees. Mixed with the sound of waves lapping the beach and a gentle sea breeze blowing in from the ocean, I thought I was waking up in Paradise! Someday, I will really enjoy waking up from a nap on the shore of the Crystal Sea to this kind of natural music.

Now, let's take a peek inside . . .

The Clothes Closet

Most bedrooms include some sort of clothes closet and/or clothes dresser. This is where most of us dress at the beginning of our day and undress at the end of our day. However, the Bible suggests we will be clothed with garments of light which, if you stop to think about it, poses some very interesting possibilities.[1]

To start with, light has absolutely no weight. Therefore, one who wore a garment of light would essentially enjoy a freedom of physical movement as if they had no clothes on at all! No buttoned, zipped, snapped, or elastic materials to bind, kink, or otherwise restrict the smooth and graceful movement of your perfect body whatsoever. How cool is that?

Light has several other intriguing properties that would be especially conducive to wearing as a garment. For instance, suppose you could change the colors, patterns, textures, and brightness of different parts of your garment of light, perhaps even at will.[2] The only limits to your wardrobe would be your own imagination. But you most certainly would not need a closet, a dresser, or a chest of drawers to store your shirts, pants, or dresses made of light.

---

[1] Matthew 17:2, 1 John 3:2, Matthew 13:43
[2] Zechariah 9:16–17 MSG

The above descriptions would also hold true for all other accessories, such as belts, hats, and shoes. But on second thought, maybe we won't need accessories for our garments of light after all. Let's think about this for a minute.

Here on the old earth, a belt is used to hold up your pants or tighten the waistline of a skirt or robe. And we use hats to shade our eyes and protect our head from sunburn, rain, and cold wind. But guess what? We won't have any of those problems while living in a perfect climate with a perfect body that is covered with perfectly form-fitted garments of light.

And as for shoes, I can't possibly imagine a reason to wear those if everything is covered in soft, luxurious green grass, fine grain, white sand, or smooth, translucent gold pavement.[3] Everything we walk on will be either soft and clean, smooth and clean, or otherwise feel just great on our perfect feet. Perfect soles for perfect souls! So, perhaps belts, hats, and shoes will not be needed with our garments of light.

Some may be wondering what kind of cleaning and care our garments of light might require. Glad you asked, because next, we are going to talk about . . .

---

[3] Revelation 21:21 KJV

The Laundry Room

Our laundry room contains the usual appliances. We have a nice automatic washing machine and clothes dryer. We also have an ironing board and a steam iron. But will we need all these labor-saving appliances to care for our garments of light? Thankfully, the answer is *no*.

Some of the most significant benefits to wearing garments of light are that they never get dirty or smell bad. Remember, a perfect climate means no dust or germs, and a perfect body means no sweat or bad bacteria. So, there goes any need for a clothes washer or dryer, along with the usual laundry soap and fabric softener. And since garments of light also never get wrinkled, we won't need an iron and ironing board. Hallelujah! So, there goes the need for a laundry room in our heavenly mansion.

However, the laundry room in our house on this old earth serves one other very important purpose. This is where our house cat's litter box is kept. This box serves as his toilet, since he produces the same bodily waste products we humans do. I've already mentioned my belief that our perfect bodies in Heaven will produce no waste materials from the food we eat, the water we drink, or the air we breathe.

By extension, it is also reasonable to assume none of God's created animals will produce waste material either. Therefore, I don't see the need for a litter box for our indoor pets, nor will we have to step carefully around the yard to avoid manure from our outdoor pets.

In fact, there will be no need at all to distinguish between indoor and outdoor pets. Want to bring your tiger inside the house for a visit? Go right ahead and enjoy the company! Want to swim with the dolphins in the Crystal Sea or soar with the eagles above a mountain top? Yes, I believe all this will be possible for the saved.

What about how obnoxious some animals smell here on earth? Well, animal odors originate with the same bad bacteria that make humans smell bad too. Since all the animals in Heaven will have perfectly clean bodies that look, feel, smell, and function just like the Master Designer originally created them, I don't believe you will need to hold your nose around them or wash your hands after petting them. In turn, they will not be plagued with fleas, ticks, flies, or any other irritating critters. So, we won't have to worry about flea collars, bug spray, or any vet bills either.

Since we are talking about domesticated *and* wild animals, I should mention one other very important thing. The Bible tells us the animals will not have to stalk, kill, and eat each other in Heaven or on the New Earth to survive.[1] Nor will any of them pose danger of any kind, even to our smallest children.[2] They will all be friendly and affectionate toward us and get along very well with each other.

However, not *every* animal that has ever existed on our planet will be in Heaven or on the New Earth. For example, consider the dinosaurs. We know for a fact they lived in fairly large numbers all over the earth before the flood. Some could fly, some could swim, and some were land-bound creatures. But we have no evidence that any were included in the ark, which the Lord commanded Noah to build. So why did the Lord exclude them?

One theory is that the dinosaurs were an *amalgamation* (confused

---

[1] Isaiah 65:25
[2] Isaiah 11:6–9 KJV

mix) of several species interbred by antediluvian scientists, and so were not part of God's original creation. Although geological evidence suggests all the dinosaurs perished in the flood, there are other amalgamated species which have survived to this very day.

Take for example, some of the truly hideous creatures occasionally captured in deep sea fishing nets. Are we to believe they will be terrorizing all the swimmers in the Crystal Sea? I think not! Contrary to what science fiction movies portray, our God never created any dangerous, horrible looking monsters or ill-tempered humanoids anywhere in the universe. The interstellar creatures you see on TV and in the movies are devil-inspired, Hollywood-manufactured distortions of God's perfect creation.

Everything God has given His breath of life to was perfectly formed in appearance and in temperament. God Himself pronounced everything He made as "good."[3] Unfortunately, when Adam and Eve believed the lies Lucifer told them about God's character,[4] everything on this earth began a long, slow process of degeneration and decay, ending in death from the curse of sin.

From the most microscopic life forms, deadly germs, viruses, and bacteria developed. From the plant kingdom, thorns, thistles, and weeds began to grow.[5] Even the climate changed. Some areas of earth produced high levels of heat and humidity, spawning terrible thunderstorms, tornadoes, hurricanes, and monsoons. Other areas were turned into hot, dry deserts or frozen arctic tundra where survival was difficult even for the hardiest animals and plants.

Most species of the animal kingdom degenerated into wild creatures using fangs, teeth, and claws on each other just to survive. Earth became one vast killing zone where animals had to eat each other just to survive. The Bible simply states that all of creation "groans and agonizes in pain" waiting to be delivered from the death sentence, which

---

[3] Genesis 1:31 KJV
[4] Genesis 3:4–5 KJV
[5] Genesis 3:17–19 KJV

separation from God brought to mankind and the animal and plant kingdoms.[6] When God remakes the New Earth, I believe He will restore all of the animals and plants to their full glory as He originally made them.

Now, let me address one other thing animal lovers frequently ask about. We wonder if God might resurrect our beloved family pets so we can have the pleasure of their company in Heaven and on the New Earth. Before we dismiss this as a foolish thought of the spiritually immature, let us remember God intentionally created *all* the animals in the original Garden of Eden as companions for Adam and Eve.[7] In fact, the Bible makes it quite clear that we are to regard the life of our animals in a personally responsible way.[8]

So, could it be that in the process of creating the animals we will enjoy in Heaven, God might also re-create our beloved pets too? I believe He can. However, I know some people may argue that animals do not have souls and therefore are not eligible for resurrection. Well, I don't know about you, but I definitely won't be trying to tell the King of the Universe whom or what He can or cannot raise on resurrection morning!

So, don't be too surprised if you are greeted at the door of your heavenly mansion or country home by a very familiar bark, meow, or whinny. We serve a delightfully detailed and thoughtful Creator. All nature abundantly testifies to this fact.

Okay, let's move on to . . .

---

[6] Romans 8:19–22 KJV
[7] Genesis 2:19–20 KJV
[8] Proverbs 12:10 KJV

The Living Room

The living room is an interesting name for a room. I always thought we were *living* in each room of our house! Well, in my living room, we have a couch for guests and a reclining chair where I take it easy when I'm tired. There are three tall bookcases holding my lifetime collection of books and a beautiful electric piano. There is also a nice warm fireplace, which is really fun to cuddle in front of with my loved ones on a cold winter night.

Before we begin to think about each of the above items and how they might fit into our heavenly mansion, let's consider some other related information. First, I firmly believe the Bible teaches we will be a social people in Heaven.[1] We won't be living in one place for years without knowing our neighbor's name. The Bible also teaches that vast multitudes of the redeemed from all nations, tribes, races, and languages will be there, all living together in perfect harmony with the angels and other unfallen beings from around the universe.[2]

Because even the streets are paved with gold,[3] I don't believe we will be separated by rich or poor neighborhoods, since economic wealth will not be needed for survival or anything else your heart may

---

[1] Colossians 3:12–14 ESV
[2] Revelation 7:9
[3] Revelation 21:21

desire. Nor will we be limited in our long-distance visitations by the usual semester and summer breaks for students, or the usual two or three weeks off from work per year. Hooray for that!

Although the Bible teaches that man was originally made a little lower than the angels,[4] it also states he will be made equal to the angels (at least, in *some* of their characteristic abilities) at the resurrection.[5] So, let's consider for a moment what the ability to *travel* like an angel might mean for us.

The Bible gives at least one documented instance of an angel being dispatched from the throne room of God and physically traveling the distance between Heaven and earth to answer a prayer *as it was spoken*.[6] So, if we are given an angel's ability to travel through space without any limitations from time or distance, then it is reasonable to assume we will be able to visit with our friends and loved ones whenever we may mutually desire, no matter where in the universe we or they might happen to be visiting or living.

With this background information in mind, I would guess there will be some sort of comfortable seating arrangements in our living room or in whatever room in our mansion we set aside for visitation.

Of course, we don't know if those seating arrangements will include a traditional bench or a couch and easy chair. It is even conceivable to think we might not need furniture at all. What if we have some soft, living, green grass to sit on beside a bubbling brook, flowing right through the middle of our house? Could it be that natural landscaping will provide some or all of the furnishings and decorations in our heavenly homes? Maybe.

But no matter how the rooms for visitation in our mansions are furnished, I sure do like the idea of being able to visit with old friends and new friends alike, as often as desired, with absolutely NO heartbreaking separations like we frequently endure here.

---

[4] Psalms 8:5 KJV
[5] Luke 20:36 KJV
[6] Daniel 9:20–23 NLT

Now, let's consider what place my book collection might have in Heaven. I may be going out on a limb here, but I don't think there will be any need for books, magazines, or other printed media there. So, what is wrong with having books in your heavenly mansion, you might ask? After all, people have used books here on this old earth for a wide variety of useful purposes over the last several centuries.

Some books are read for the pure enjoyment of sharing the stories, drama, and history of our fellow human beings. And some books are used to educate our minds, enhance our talents, and spark our imaginations with new knowledge, concepts, and ideas. Other books are used for reference purposes since we can't possibly know or remember everything about everything. And of course, the Bible is the story of the great controversy between good and evil, between Christ and Satan. And it is His word to us right now.

But what if you had a truly photographic mind? Suppose you could clearly and distinctly remember each and every single detail of *everything* you *ever* saw, heard, smelled, tasted, felt, or experienced through any of your greatly enhanced senses. And just suppose those memories came with lightning recall and total clarity, no matter how many years, centuries, or millenniums passed. Wouldn't that be simply awesome?

If this were the case, there would be no need for any kind of reference books, magazines, or photo albums, which make up most of what is on my bookcases right now. Your mind would be so much better than all the encyclopedias, all the internet search engines, and all the accumulated wisdom of each specialty field on this present earth, *all put together*!

And think about how going to school would be forever changed from a fatiguing chore into an exhilarating and satisfying adventure filled with the exploration of God's whole universe. From the smallest atoms to the greatest worlds, there would be absolutely nothing beyond your mental power to grasp, thoroughly understand, and remember completely in every detail forever.

For example, suppose you wanted to learn about a new planet

you've never seen or been to before. How about experiencing a new culture you've just learned about? Why not visit in person and stay as long as you want? You will be perfectly welcome and feel completely safe and at home anywhere in God's great universe.

Want to master a new skill or invent a new technology to build or accomplish something you've never done before? Just find a master craftsman on the New Earth, or on one of the unfallen worlds, and ask. You will not need to write down directions or enter numbers into a database, word processor, or spreadsheet to record or calculate what it all means. You will remember every single detail of your conversation better than if you had a video recorder. And most importantly, you'll have all the time, patience, physical dexterity, and mental energy you could possibly need for the most amazing results imaginable.

Suppose you wanted to explore all the realms of science and have adventures of all kinds within the three dimensions of time, space, and matter we currently know about. And what about exploring other dimensions of existence we can't even begin to imagine right now? Just ask the Master Designer, who created all the scientific laws and principles of biology, chemistry, and physics in operation throughout every dimension of existence within the entire universe.

Maybe you wanted to learn more about a Bible story or some event in history from the old earth. You won't need to look it up in a dusty old encyclopedia or parse through a million hits on a search engine. Instead, you'll find someone who was actually there and get an exciting, first-person account of what really happened.

I'm sure you are beginning to see just some of the truly unlimited possibilities available to the saved for learning and experiencing exciting and totally satisfying new things. These learning opportunities will infinitely exceed what our finest schools, libraries, laboratories, and the internet combined can provide now.

So, I just don't believe there will be any need to have bookcases filled with books, magazines, or computer software just to learn or reference what interests you. Instead, you will be able to experience everything God has created in His vast, beautiful universe live, up close and in person!

How about that?

Now, let's consider my electric piano. I'm sure all of us will be blessed with a wide variety of tremendously expanded talents for singing, playing, and composing music. And I believe many of the fine musical instruments invented here will be made and tuned to perfection in Heaven for making joyful music to the glory of God and in harmony with the angelic choirs, orchestras, and bands. There might even be entirely new classes of instruments, which produce sounds and harmony we can hardly image right now.

Personally, I've always been totally fascinated with the majestic sound of a large, well-designed, and well-played pipe organ, placed in an acoustically designed setting. So, one of my goals in Heaven will be to build the largest pipe organ in the whole universe, put it in a pitch-perfect location, and then learn how to play it really well. Is this what some might call a *pipe dream*? Just kidding!

Okay, now what about our living room fireplace? Well, one thing is for certain. We won't be needing one to keep us warm during a long, cold winter night, because there won't be any of those in Heaven or on the New Earth. How is that possible, you may ask?

Well, I surely don't have all the answers, but the Bible does indicate that the sun and moon will both be considerably brighter than they are now. I have also heard some rather intriguing theories of how a water vapor-based canopy, high in the atmosphere, could be used to even out light and heat all around our planet from a brighter sun and moon. Well, that will certainly put a new *light* on things!

There are several more issues to consider while talking about a fireplace. Yes, burning wood produces heat, which we have used down through history to produce warmth and cook food. But before you can burn any wood, you must first chop down and cut up a living tree. I personally find it very hard to imagine the sound of axes, chain saws, and bulldozers tearing up the magnificent forests of Heaven and the

New Earth. And I simply can't imagine a huge logging truck hurtling down the streets of gold to a sawmill.

Beyond all that comes the problem of air pollution in the form of smoke and soot, which comes from the combustion process of burning wood. Do we really want smoke pollution obscuring the view around our heavenly home? Of course not! Although I'm not sure what we will have there to create the wonderful ambiance of a fireplace, I *am* sure it will not require the destruction of our living trees nor generate any air pollution.

One other thing I forgot to mention in my living room. There are lots of family photos. Now, why do we create, frame, and keep family photos anyway? Well, if your family is living with you, those photos serve as reminders of shared times of joy or accomplishment we like to remember and share with others. And if your family lives some distance away from you, those photos mean even more.

But if your cherished family members are dead, those photographs might be your only way to remember them with any detail. However, you can be absolutely certain that in Heaven, death, time, and distance will *never* keep us from actually being present with our loved ones in person the very instant we want their company.

How about traveling anywhere in the universe at the speed of thought? Yes, this will be possible for God's people then, just like it is for the angels now. But possessing a photographic memory of exactly how our loved ones look, feel, smell, and sound will probably make it completely unnecessary to have any photographs of them on our walls.

So, what other kinds of decorations will be on the inside walls of our heavenly mansions in the New Jerusalem, or our country homes on the New Earth? I honestly don't know. But I DO know that all nature demonstrates our Creator's abilities as a Master Designer and Decorator with an absolutely perfect sense of style, shape, color, texture, symmetry, beauty, balance, and function. I really don't think He will have any challenges whatsoever showing us the endless possibilities for personalizing our homes with decorations that will be breathtakingly beautiful, completely satisfying, and immensely practical.

Now, let's move on to . . .

The Kitchen

The kitchen has traditionally been the heart of most family homes. It is where meals are prepared, and the dining table is often located here as well. Many of us have fond memories of the great smells and delicious food, along with interesting conversations and laughter emanating from the kitchens in our past.

The kitchen in our home is no exception. Ours has many modern, labor-saving devices designed for cooking, storing, and preserving food. These appliances are necessary because some foods must be heated before they are safe to eat, while other foods must be cooled or frozen to preserve freshness.

Our kitchen also includes an assortment of cabinets and drawers for storing items needed to cook and eat our food. We also have a sink with fresh, running water to help us clean up after our meals are done. Finally, we have a kitchen trashcan to dispose of the cans, bottles, and boxes most food and drink items are packaged in.

Now, let's think carefully about whether or not any of these items might be needed in our heavenly kitchen. We will start with the kitchen trash can. It probably won't be needed at all because our food will come from totally fresh, clean, renewable resources. There will be no bones, gristle, fat, skins, peelings, or packaging of any kind to throw away.

Based on God's description of Adam and Eve's original diet in the Garden of Eden,[1] we can only assume we will eat a fruit-and-nut-based diet and drink in moderation just what we need to sustain a healthy, energetic lifestyle, with nothing left over to throw away. Without a doubt, there will be no need for slaughterhouses, garbage cans, dumpsters, trash trucks, or landfills anywhere in Heaven.

And yet, the Bible makes it abundantly clear we will all enjoy partaking of *real* food and drink in Heaven, including fruit from the Tree of Life.[2] We also know there are other kinds of food in Heaven, which are not currently present on earth. For example, ever hear of manna?[3] It is a safe bet we will get to sample many new and delicious kinds of food and drink from the enormous variety of cultures on the unfallen worlds throughout God's great universe.

Although we cannot be sure exactly how heavenly foods and drinks will be prepared, we can be certain that heat, refrigeration, or freezing will not be specifically required to preserve anything we eat or drink. This is because harmful bacteria and germs will no longer be present after sin is destroyed. Consequently, there will be no need for expiration labels or food preservatives. But since even some natural foods taste better when cooled, warmed, mixed, or baked, we can't rule out some sort of devices for these tasks.

As for how we clean up the items we cook and eat with after a meal, we can only imagine some possibilities. Perhaps there will be a shallow, sunlit stream of crystal-clear water flowing right through the middle of our kitchen where we can put items to be cleaned in the most natural way possible. I don't know for sure.

But one thing I *am* sure of—it will be a *lot* of fun to find out firsthand just how a meal is prepared, served, and shared in Heaven. Without a doubt, our greatly enhanced senses will be thoroughly delighted by the sight, taste, and smell of everything on our table in Heaven

---

[1] Genesis 1:29 KJV
[2] Isaiah 25:6–8 MSG, Luke 22:30 KJV, Revelation 2:7 KJV
[3] Exodus 16:31 KJV

and on the New Earth. Picky eaters, rejoice! We will all have plenty of good, wholesome, tasty food and drink for ourselves, and to share with our loved ones and friends.

And this brings our discussion to . . .

The Dining Room

One of the greatest joys in Heaven will be our social life. God created within each one of us a strong desire to share close companionship and friendship. What better place to share with family and friends than over a good meal, with some fine background music in a comfortable dining room?

What about the conversations we will have around the dining room table there? Do you suppose we will all have to learn to think and speak in a new language? As you may recall from the biblical story about the Tower of Babel, everyone on earth spoke the same language until God found it necessary to confuse their languages.[1]

Of course, since written records were not kept (or needed!) then, we have no way of knowing what the pre- and post-flood language was. But apparently, it was the same verbal language God placed within the brains of Adam and Eve when He created them. Remember, they are the only two humans who were never born or raised as children. God created them as young adults with fully developed verbal and non-verbal languages. So, it is logical to assume that all the saved will speak the same language in Heaven that Adam and Eve once spoke on earth.

Therefore, I don't believe we will have any language barriers to deal

---

[1] Genesis 11:9 KJV

with after the resurrection. Nor do I believe we will have any problem communicating in a personal way with any member of the Trinity or any of the angels.

The only real language questions I wonder about are what other forms of communication are in use on the multitudes of unfallen worlds scattered around God's universe. Do they use verbal and/or non-verbal forms of communication like we do? Or can some of God's created beings actually utilize mental telepathy to communicate sensory details we can't even begin to describe with our current verbal languages? It will be so much fun to travel around each galaxy and experience the answers to these intriguing questions in person. I can hardly wait!

Now, let's move on to . . .

The Office

The office is where my wife and I keep our computers, desks, file cabinets, and assorted office equipment. So, let's start with our computers. The smartest living human beings today have certified IQs ranging from 190 to 228+.[1] And yet, many believe even the gifted are using only about one-tenth of their total brain capacity. What if we could harness *all* of the brain power God originally gave Adam and Eve?

Just imagine if your mind had a 2,000 IQ, along with a photographic memory to match. What need would we *ever* have for a computer? Without a doubt, God's people will *never* have to worry about their brains getting tired, overwhelmed, or unable to remember, comprehend, or apply knowledge and skills on the very highest levels of mental achievement.

And while we are on the subject of computers, what about the internet? In our modern world, the internet is used to transfer all kinds of information for virtually every business, industry, and institution you can think of. But in Heaven and on the New Earth, can you imagine any real need to send or receive data electronically? Let's take a quick look at just a few scenarios, and I think you will see what I mean.

---

[1] https://www.scienceabc.com/humans/who-are-some-of-the-people-with-the-highest-iq.html

Banking: Since we will all have access to unlimited material resources, there is no need whatsoever for a monetary-based economy. Therefore, no one needs to earn money, save money, spend money, or borrow money for anything they could possibly want or need. So, there is no need to trade financial or credit data.

Insurance: Everyone lives for all eternity in a completely healthy, safe environment. So, nobody needs life, health, accident, or disability insurance. And your heavenly mansion or country home on the New Earth will never need any fire, theft, flood, or liability insurance either. So, no need to trade insurance data.

Healthcare: Nobody dies, gets sick, injured, or goes crazy. So, no need to trade physical or mental health data.

Legal: Nobody is divorced, sued, prosecuted, fined, or jailed. So, no need to trade any legal or criminal data.

Education: Nobody struggles for an education or has to provide a certification for employment. So, no need to trade academic transcripts, diplomas, certifications, or student loan data. Yay!

Government: Nobody runs for office, levies taxes, or formulates national or foreign policies. So, there will be no need for any of the myriads of government data functions we currently depend on.

Military: There is NO Army, Navy, Air Force, Marines, Coast Guard, FBI, CIA, or any police force there. So, no need for any type of military communications or security monitoring at all.

Social Media: Why would you ever visit over a webcam or cell phone or send an email or text message when you can visit in person the very instant you want? I predict there will be no need whatsoever for any kind of social media in Heaven. We will all enjoy instant, in-person, social communication with our loved ones and friends, anytime, anywhere we mutually wish.

Entertainment: Do you *really* think there will be boom-boom radios, profane television and theater, or obscene internet streaming anywhere in Heaven or on the New Earth? No, no, and NO! Enough said.

What about the electricity that powers our computers, servers, and networks? Well, God *is* the original inventor of electricity. Who do you think created the electrical properties of protons, electrons, and neutrons, as well as lightening, the aurora borealis, and static electricity? However, I'm still not sure if our heavenly mansions will have electrical outlets. Let's think about this one for a few moments.

What do we use electricity for in the house? Lighting, heating, cooling, cooking, running electronics of all kinds. But will we have an actual need for *any* of this technology in Heaven? Probably not, as we have already discussed several of these items previously. By extension, I think you will come to the same conclusions I have. We truly won't need or miss *any* of these modern, labor-saving devices in our heavenly mansions or in our country homes either.

What about all the infrastructure needed to deliver electricity to your home? Do you really expect to see power poles on either side of the streets of gold, with power lines snaking their way all over the New Jerusalem? And will we have large power plants belching smoke or radiation up into the atmosphere? Or will there be a large hydro-electric dam backing up all the water in the River of Life to churn out a few megawatts of electricity? I think not!

Well, what about clean energy sources, such as wind power and solar cells? Since I happen to like windmills, I won't attempt to discourage the idea of some form of wind-driven energy sources in Heaven or on the New Earth. But, as for solar cells, they are certainly great, except when you start thinking about all the labor and raw materials that must go into their manufacturing.

I don't want to be dogmatic here, because I *do* believe there will be *many* forms of clean, safe, dependable energy available in unlimited abundance, which doesn't depend on any technology we have in existence today. What other kinds of energy could there be? How would we harness it, and for what purposes? The answers to these questions would stretch the thoughts of every chemist, physicist, and inventor on earth today. A 2,000+ IQ might be necessary to function in Heaven after all!

But may I suggest that something as small as a microscopic atom could hold a great deal of energy? If rightly understood and used, it could provide abundant power in many dimensions of time and space we simply are not capable of comprehending at the present time with our limited IQ. And what about all the energy found in solar radiation, planetary magnetic fields, or in gravity itself?

The point is this: I believe our God will show us just how to generate any kind of power we need or want, to build or accomplish absolutely anything we can dream up. More importantly, we will be able to generate and use this power without endangering ourselves or the environment God created for us in the process. So, fellow environmentalists, rejoice—Heaven and the New Earth will definitely be our kind of places!

Let's return to my office and talk about how my wife and I use our office desks and file cabinets. In our home, we use these items to help organize and store our bills and other important records for easy access. But let's think about why we do this and consider if we would need to do the same thing there.

In Heaven and on the New Earth, *none* of us will have *any* utility bills, mortgage or automobile payments, or insurance payments. We won't have any withholdings for Social Security, Medicare, Medicaid, or Federal and State income taxes (at long last—hooray!). There will be no credit card payments, medical bills, rent, or lease payments. No check book to balance, no stocks and bonds to trade, no retirement funds to manage. So, what need will we have for a desk, file cabinets, or computers to store our various financial records? None, I say, and good riddance to all of them.

But now, what about our office trash can? It contains mostly paper products, such as junk mail, old newspapers and magazines, sales receipts, and old bills and records that are shredded and no longer needed. The typical North American family throws away *so* much trash that most cities and suburbs have to utilize large garbage trucks to collect the trash from every home and business at least once a week.

And where do those garbage trucks go? To enormous landfills on the outskirts of cities and towns all over the planet.

Personally, I find it difficult to believe there will be *any* trash products of any kind in Heaven or on the New Earth. Of course, living trash-free will require a radical transformation in nearly every area of how we live because, let's face it, just about everything we do in this present life produces some kind of trash, waste product, or leftovers. Just imagining the possibilities of a completely trash- and waste-free existence will give you "food for thought" for a long time!

Okay, now let's talk about . . .

The Garage

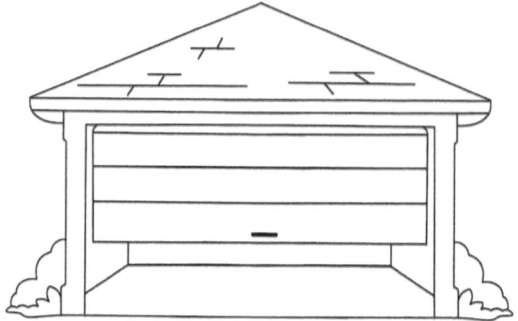

The garage is the last "room" in my house I will talk about. This is where most people park their cars, keep their yard tools, and store unneeded items. To care for the yard around my house, I require the use of a lawn mower, weed-eater, leaf blower, pressure washer, and various gardening hand tools.

Honestly, I can't imagine having to mow the grass every week around my heavenly mansion or country home! Perhaps the grass in our yards will be genetically engineered to grow just a certain height and then stop growing. Who knows for sure? But one thing *is* for certain. We will not have any weeds to pull, nor will we have fallen trees, broken branches, or dead leaves to remove from our properties. Even the trees and plants live forever there.

What about our cars? I'm glad you asked! In North America, a wide variety of cars, trucks, motorcycles, buses, subways, monorails, and trains provide ground transportation to move people to work and to school. They also move cargo between factories and stores all around our nation. However, most of these modern vehicles burn copious amounts of fossil fuels in the form of gasoline, diesel fuel, or kerosene to power their engines.

As the name implies, fossil fuels are made from the fossilized remains of vast forests that covered our planet before the flood. Of course, the formation of a fossil requires a tree or plant to die in order to eventually become fossilized. Since no plant or animal has ever died anywhere else in the entire universe, except right here on planet Earth, it is safe to say we have the only fossil fuel supply in all of creation. Since God will destroy our old earth with fire, and then re-create it from the inside out, I don't think there will be any fossil fuels remaining on the New Earth.

The Bible indicates there will be nothing in Heaven or on the New Earth to pollute the environment.[1] This would seem to eliminate all of our current methods of ground transportation as well as all aircraft and most ships (excluding sailing vessels, of course) from being present there. So, just how will we all get around? Well, let me answer that question by asking a few other questions, just to get your imagination going.

Have you ever watched how a big bird glides and soars effortlessly alone or in formation with other birds through the sky? Ever wanted to do the same thing, only without all the noise and vibration of a modern airplane or helicopter? You may be wondering just how we will be able to do that since it is well beyond our current abilities to defy gravity without some sort of artificial means of lift and propulsion.

However, the Bible describes angels both hovering and flying through the sky, as well as traversing the vast distance between Heaven and earth very quickly in answer to prayer.[2] So, let's use our *deductive* reasoning powers and think about what the Bible says about angels.

Jesus said, at the resurrection we would be "like the angels."[3] It is important to note that He didn't say we would actually *be* angels, but that we would be *like* the angels. I believe this means we will share at least *some* of their characteristic abilities, one being their ability to fly through the atmosphere and outer space without any visible means of artificial life support or propulsion.

---

[1] Revelation 21:27
[2] Daniel 9:20–23
[3] Matthew 22:29–30, Mark 12:24–25

So, what if you wanted to fly over the treetops like a bird, float slowly over the fields or meadows like a butterfly, or soar over the highest mountains and through the deepest canyons like an eagle? And suppose you wanted to play tag with your friends around some puffy cumulus clouds at the speed of a small plane. That would be fun! There might be other times you would want to pick up the pace and streak across the sky like a modern jet plane, complete with contrails.

Or maybe it would thrill you to take off from the ground straight up like a rocket, right out into space where you could see the magnificent curvature of the earth itself. Yes, that would be awe inspiring! Or perhaps you would like to take an interplanetary tour of our solar system, walk on the moon, see if anyone actually lives on Mars, or hitch a ride on a comet around the sun. I'm sure you are beginning to get the picture.

Now, suppose you wanted to move between our solar system and some of the nearby star systems in the Milky Way Galaxy. Just like the angels, you would no longer be bound by the laws of biology, chemistry, and physics, which our current three dimensions of time, space, and matter force us to obey.

And this brings up the ultimate form of transportation—travel at the speed of thought. You merely think about where you want to be, and you are there! As demonstrated by the Old Testament stories of angels being dispatched from the throne of God to answer a prayer *while it was being spoken*, I believe moving from place to place like this will be a very real possibility for God's children.[4]

I also firmly believe God will provide infinitely more enjoyable, safe, and practical methods of getting around Heaven and, in fact, the entire universe, than we have here on this old earth. So, in short, I don't think our heavenly mansion or our country estate on the New Earth will have any need of a garage for cars, or even a barn for horses and buggies, unless of course, that is your thing!

---

[4] Daniel 9:20–23

Now, we will expand the scope of our discussion from our house to our community.

43

PART III
OUR COMMUNITY

Now that we have finished exploring my house and comparing its contents to what we might or might not expect to find in our heavenly homes, let's widen our circle. Let's explore my neighborhood, and then the nearby city. We will follow the same pattern of *deductive* and *inferential* reasoning for what we experience with our various senses to explore the question of whether or not it would make any sense to want or need the same things in the New Jerusalem of Heaven or anywhere else on the New Earth.

The Neighborhood

One of my children's favorite TV shows featured healthy interactions between wholesome guests from a wide variety of interesting occupations. The setting was usually in a typical middle-class neighborhood. Unfortunately, neighbors in many modern cultures rarely interact anymore. Adults are just too busy earning a living and getting ahead with their careers. And children are just too busy with after-school activities to visit with their neighbors like they used to in times past. Nowadays, most of us could not name who lives within a one-block radius of our homes.

This will definitely *not* be the case in Heaven or on the New Earth. I'm not sure just how close our city mansions and country homes will be spaced there. But I firmly believe we will never have to deal with all the negatives generated by high-density housing projects and apartment complexes ever again. Heaven will be a spacious place filled with all races of people pleasantly interacting in a beautiful, natural setting. There, our lives will be completely free from the noise and frantic pressures of our fast-paced modern lifestyle.

In our current neighborhood, we have some very fine public and private schools from kindergarten to a graduate-level university. We also have beautiful parks, playgrounds, and sports complexes. We even have miles of well-maintained greenways, bike paths, and nature trails. It is a safe, quiet, clean place to live, and it's close to plentiful shopping and employment. In short, our neighborhood is about as pleasant as this old earth currently offers. But all these things pale into near total insignificance compared to the splendors awaiting the saved.

I have already mentioned how different I would expect the schools of Heaven to be for God's people, both children and adults. But we haven't explored one subject, which is near and dear to the heart of many Christians today and down through history. And that subject is sports. On our present earth, virtually all sports can be divided into two basic categories: contact and non-contact.

Contact sports involve strategic planning for the tactical use of physical force to overwhelm your opponent. Personally, I find it hard to believe there would be any contact sports in Heaven, where the stronger would be pitted against the weaker, and where there would always be a winner and a loser. I also can't imagine an audience wildly cheering on for their favorite teams or throwing temper tantrums over a coach's decision or a referee's call.

Non-contact sports involve a competition of acquired skills, many of which have historically been featured in the Olympic games. But since competition of any kind still results in a winner and a loser, maybe the human concept of competition itself will have to be changed. If this is the case, I see no reason why we couldn't all enjoy the potential physical and social benefits of these activities.

But just like anything else we care to name, if God takes away something we enjoy in this present life, He will definitely replace it with something better in the life to come. You can count on that! You can also rest completely assured that *all* of God's people will be winners in Heaven for all eternity.

The *only* real losers in the whole universe will be Lucifer, his demon angels, and those humans who have forced themselves physically, mentally, emotionally, sexually, financially, or spiritually on the weak.[1] God guarantees we will all be forever safe from any form of bullying, abuse, or exploitation. In fact, the Bible says the wicked will be as ashes beneath our feet on the New Earth.[2] Talk about the ultimate payback!

As we drive around our local neighborhood, we notice a large number of churches, bearing the signs of many different denominations and faiths. This brings up an interesting question. Will there be any churches in Heaven or on the New Earth, and if so, which ones? Well, let's think about this intriguing question.

Why do we go to church? The primary reason the Bible tells us not to forsake the assembling of ourselves together is because corporate worship fulfills an important need we have to praise God *with* fellow believers.[3] We can also give and receive a lot of encouragement, which serves to strengthen all of us in the daily battles we each face while living on this old sinful world.

We seek God's guidance and blessing *together* through our prayers. We praise God *together* through our songs and instrumental music. And we learn about God *together* through the hearing, studying, and discussing of His word. We also practice good stewardship by pooling our financial resources *together* to support the ministry of God's church. And finally, it pleases God when we graciously share fellowship *together* with members and visitors alike. Now, let's think about what "church" might look like in Heaven.

The Bible paints a panoramic picture of corporate worship each Sabbath in Heaven.[4] Human beings, angels, and sentient beings from the unfallen worlds will all assemble to praise God with voice and instrumental music. So, the pleasure of singing and playing music to the glory of God will be one aspect of our current worship service that will definitely be found in Heaven.

---

[1] Ezekiel 28:18
[2] Malachi 4:3
[3] Hebrews 10:25
[4] Isaiah 66:23

But the worship and praise given to God from the saved of earth will have a distinctly unique sweetness to God's ears. This is because we will be the only one's present who know firsthand what it means to be ransomed from sin, sickness, sorrow, and death. The songs we sing then will have a much more powerful and personal meaning than anything we could sing now, because we will be eternally free at last from the curse of separation from our Creator.

The Bible also says we will no longer have a veil between us and any member of the Trinity.[5] In other words, we will be able to walk and talk with them at any time we desire. For this reason, I don't believe we will have any further need for prayer.

To illustrate what I mean, answer this question: When was the last time you bowed your head and closed your eyes when walking or talking with a friend or a loved one? Most of us prefer to *look* at the person we are communicating with, because facial expressions and body language greatly enhance our ability to understand and appreciate what the other is saying. The saved will experience that level of intimacy with each member of the Trinity, which will be truly awesome and enjoyed to the highest degree imaginable.

I doubt we will have any need for hymnals or any kind of sheet music either, since we will all be blessed with photographic memories and incredibly expanded instrumental and singing skills. We probably won't even carry a Bible there, because most of the Bible characters will be present with us in Heaven. Why read about their adventures when you can hear all about it straight from the very ones who lived it, with exponentially greater background, detail, and insight than was recorded in the Bible?

Now, let's consider our tithes and offerings for a moment. Tithes are primarily given to support our ministers, missionaries, and teachers. Offerings are typically used to build and maintain church, school, and hospital buildings, and to provide community services to the poor.

---

[5] I Corinthians 13:12

However, there will be *no* poor people to help, no sick people, elderly shut-ins, or incarcerated prisoners to visit. There also won't be any ministers, evangelists, or missionaries to support. Nor will there be any church, school, or hospital buildings to pay for or maintain.

In fact, as I've already mentioned, I don't think there will be any use for money in Heaven or on the New Earth at all. What need is there for money when everyone already has an unlimited supply of every resource they could possibly need or want? I really think this is the true meaning behind the Bible's description of the streets of gold.[6] It is just a common paving material to walk on in Heaven!

One more important thing to consider about churches. They are supposed to be places to bring people to Christ. But remember, there are *no* sinners anywhere in the whole universe, after the devil and his followers are eternally destroyed.[7] So, there are no more people to convert and baptize. Those who were ministers and missionaries on this old earth will be completely out of their traditional "work" in Heaven. But I bet they won't mind it one bit!

---

[6] Revelation 21:21
[7] Malachi 4:1

The City

We are now leaving our clean, quiet, suburban neighborhood and are cruising smoothly down the highway toward our nearest city. As we get closer to our destination, we notice the level of traffic beginning to rise dramatically. Then suddenly, our smooth highway cruise has turned into a bumper-to-bumper traffic jam. This is a very common frustration experienced daily by many commuters all over the world.

Eventually, we make it into our local city. As we drive around, we notice it is blessed with many beautiful natural attractions including hills, rivers, and parks. And parts of our city have some truly outstanding science, educational, and cultural centers. Business and manufacturing opportunities are bountiful in most areas too.

But as we continue to cruise around town, we can't help but notice some communities with rundown housing projects and multitudes of abandoned businesses and factories. We see trash in the streets and vulgar graffiti spray painted on many structures. Rest assured that none of these plagues will ever be found in the New Jerusalem or in any other city, no matter where you travel in all of God's beautiful, clean universe. Everything He creates illustrates the value He places on order and organization.

If we took the time to visit some of earth's larger cities, we would experience much higher levels of traffic and economic despair than we have in our local city. And if we visited most any large city in a third-world nation, we would undoubtedly experience negative sensory overload from sights, sounds, and smells God *never* intended for any human being to endure.

The middle of virtually *any* large city generates a lot of noise. Cars, buses, and trucks with engines revving, brakes squeaking, and horns blowing. Rumbling sounds from trains, subways, and monorails vibrating the ground. And then there are the incessant sirens and alarms of all kinds screaming near and far at all hours of the day and night.

And yet, multiple millions of city dwellers get so used to these noises that they hardly even notice them anymore. Some people actually get to the point where they can't stand any silence or even the quiet, natural sounds God made for us to enjoy in nature. Worse yet, many people get *so* hardened to all the noise around them, they can't stand the "sound" of their own conscience.

I'm sure there will be a pleasant background of sound from the intelligent activity of happy people and gentle animals interacting together in the New Jerusalem. But I simply cannot imagine God, the angels, or beings from other worlds putting up with the excessive noise levels generated by cities on earth today.

Next on the list of undesirable observations is the obnoxious smell and inevitable pollution generated in many high-density cities. Clouds of diesel exhaust, overflowing trash dumpsters, belching factory smokestacks, and stagnant, slime-choked waterways are common. As a direct consequence, respiratory illnesses and asthmas of all kinds are endured by millions of big-city dwellers.

Hand in hand with all the noise, bad smells, air, and water pollution are multitudes of people, cars, and buildings jammed so close together there's hardly room for movement without getting in someone's way or on someone's nerves. People using public transportation wait in endless lines to board taxis, buses, trains, subways, and planes. Others lose countless hours of productivity due to slow-moving rush-hour traffic.

Frustrations build, which negatively affect one's health. And tempers boil over so frequently, there is a term for it—road rage. I'm sure you get the picture! God never intended men and women to move around and work all jammed together in high-density offices, factories, and housing. Yet this "picture of civilization" is what we commonly find in most big cities around the world today.

Unfortunately, one of the results of living this way is a *lot* of criminal activity. Gang warfare, indiscriminate killings, and frequent extortion of business owners have become commonplace in large cities. Even in smaller towns, we hear about heartless kidnappings, unconscionable rapes, and rampant theft of all kinds. The list of crimes invented by godless people to commit against innocent men, women, and children is virtually endless.

If all this depresses you, I've got some really good news to share. Once this Great Controversy between Christ and Satan is finished, there will be only one simple equation to fully describe this subject. No sinners + No temptations = No crime to worry about ever again *anywhere* in God's perfect universe. Case closed!

Now, we will consider a small sampling of the various buildings we commonly see in a city and again use our *deductive* and *inferential* reasoning skills to figure out if it really makes any sense at all to want or need the same facilities in the New Jerusalem.

Police Station: Since there are *no* physical threats or criminal activity whatsoever, this eliminates the need for police stations, jails, prisons, lawyers' offices, or court houses. You will also never see any city police, county sheriff, or state trooper cars patrolling the streets of gold in the New Jerusalem.

Fire Station: No one needs to be rescued from a burning building or transported to the emergency room from an accident. God's kingdom is so safe you will never see an ambulance, rescue squad, or funeral hearse. Also, no need for ranger stations, forest-fire fighters, or rescue helicopters. You won't even see a lifeguard tower on the Crystal Sea beach or by the River of Life.

Military Bases: You won't see any Army troops marching or tanks drilling. You won't see any Navy ships or submarines patrolling the Crystal Sea. You won't see any Air Force fighters or bombers streaking through the skies. There will be no Marines conducting amphibious landings on the Crystal Sea Beach.

No military research facilities working round the clock to design, build, and test ever more powerful weapons of mass destruction. In fact, there will be NO wars, rumors of war, or threats of war. As a byproduct, there will be no more orphanages, prisoner-of-war camps, refugee camps, or dealing with immigration authorities.

Hospitals: You will not see any hospitals, urgent care clinics, doctor's offices, lab, or radiology facilities. No pharmaceutical factories or drug stores either. Dental, optometric, and prosthetic offices will not be found. And you definitely won't see nursing homes, rehabilitation hospitals, or mental health facilities in the New Jerusalem or anywhere on the New Earth.

However, we will all be living in a "long-term care" facility. That is precisely what Heaven and the New Earth are all about. As the old saying goes, "Working for the Lord doesn't pay much, but the retirement plan is simply out of this world!"

Cemeteries: You will never see a cemetery or funeral home anywhere in the whole universe. In fact, the Bible promises there will NEVER again be any death or decay found anywhere in the plant or animal kingdoms for the rest of eternity.

This means you will not see any fallen trees, rotting logs, or burned-out forests. All rot, mold, mildew, and germs will be eternally gone. There will be no humans hunting animals, no animals hunting humans, no humans hunting humans, or animals hunting animals. Nor will any of God's creatures be led to a slaughterhouse or be crushed and torn by the side of the road.

There definitely won't be any slimy covering of algae choking the River of Life. Nor will you find any kind of cold, black muck on the bottom of the Crystal Sea or dead fish floating on top of the water.

Nature will at last be forever free from the curse of sin, sickness, disease, and death, just like the saved children of God.

To conclude our discussion of cities, let's take a brief look at a description given in the Bible of the New Jerusalem. Found in Revelation 21:16, most translations of this verse describe the City of God as having a base perimeter of about 1,500 miles square, which would make each side about 375 miles long. Simple math will tell you that a city with those dimensions would have a base surface area of just over 140,000 square miles. By way of comparison, this would be larger than the total land area of Georgia, Tennessee, and South Carolina *combined*! Yes, there will be plenty of room in Heaven for the saved from all the nations of history to have many acres of land.

But there is much more! This verse also describes the *height* of the city as being *equal* to its length and width. In other words, John the Revelator is saying the City of God is also about 375 miles *high*. This means the city would top out about 100 miles higher than the current orbit of the International Space Station. Now, whether this dimension refers to the height of some structures or a mountain inside the city, the habitable atmosphere, or the top perimeter of the walls, we don't know. Some believe the twelve foundations of the wall, which John the Revelator talks about in Revelation 21:14, might actually represent twelve individual floors or levels *within* the Holy City. If this is true, then the city would be shaped like a truly massive cube.

These "floors" would multiply the 140,000-square-mile base area of the city by a factor of twelve, giving a total surface area of about 1.7 million square miles, which would be considerably larger than the entire land surface area of India. And if they are spaced vertically an equal distance apart, that would provide over thirty-one *miles* of atmosphere for each floor. In turn, this would give plenty of room for a different climate on each level within the city itself, complete with appropriate land and water features to meet every taste. Wow!

No matter how the City of God is shaped or constructed, these dimensions really *do* stretch the imagination! But John the Revelator states in Revelation 21:15 that he was an eyewitness to an angel who was doing the measuring. So, believe it or not, there you have a description of the New Jerusalem, which truly boggles the mind.

PART IV
OUR ATTITUDES

Now that we have finished exploring what we might or might not find in our heavenly community, we will next consider something else we won't have to put up with there either. And that is negative human attitudes of any kind!

The Holy Scriptures give many examples of the difference one's attitude can make to our sense of happiness and well-being, especially when it comes to communicating with and relating to others. But it is also a major determining factor in our relationship with God, as we shall soon see.

Fitting In with the Family of God

To understand where negative human attitudes come from, we must go all the way back in time to a point before our little world was even created. This is because the father of all negative attitudes was Lucifer the Archangel, better known today as Satan the devil.[1]

Lucifer was the highest *created* being in God's whole universe. And as such, he was endowed with great beauty, exceptional leadership skills, and tremendous musical talents.[2] In short, he was greatly beloved and respected by all of the other angels.

We don't know how long he held this position. Ezekiel 28:15 simply states that he was "perfect in all his ways, until iniquity was found in him." The word *iniquity* is a fancy way of saying that Lucifer began nurturing some really bad attitudes. Essentially, Lucifer became very jealous of the position the Son of God had as a member of the Trinity.

The Bible gives us a few clues as to where Lucifer's bad attitudes originated. Ezekiel 28:17 says that by reason of his *pride*, *intellect*, and *beauty*, he deceived himself into thinking that he could (and should!) be equal to, or greater than, the Son of God. Evidently, Lucifer chose to ignore two very important, unchangeable facts. 1) He was a *created* being. 2) Christ was his *Creator*.

In the process of deceiving himself and many other angels, Lucifer broke all of God's eternal laws, which were later codified for us as the Ten Commandments.[3] To summarize the pertinent parts:

1st Commandment—*You shall have no other gods before Me.*

Obviously, this would include Lucifer thinking that he could be equal to or greater than God.[4]

---

[1] Revelation 12:9
[2] Ezekiel 28:12–19
[3] Exodus 20:3–17
[4] Isaiah 14:13–14

2nd Commandment—*You shall not bow down to any idols.*

This would include trying to make others bow down to you as if you were a divine being, as Lucifer wanted.[5]

3rd Commandment—*You shall not misuse the name of God.*

This would include deliberately misrepresenting His character to others, as Lucifer did when deceiving the angels and Eve.[6]

4th Commandment—*Remember the Sabbath Day, to keep it holy.*

As detailed in the remainder of this commandment, one of the major purposes of Sabbath observance is to periodically acknowledge God as the Creator and Sustainer of all life. As such, He richly deserves our supreme worship, praise, and honor. But somehow, Lucifer lost sight of these facts when he refused to worship God and reverence His commandments.[7]

5th Commandment—*Honor and respect your father and mother.*

Lucifer refused to honor and respect his heavenly Father.[8]

6th Commandment—*You shall not murder.*

The Bible says there was "war in heaven."[9] Generally speaking, whoever starts a war intends to kill the opponent. Lucifer wanted his way, even to the point of having Jesus Christ and multiple millions of His followers put to death.[10]

7th Commandment—*You shall not commit adultery.*

Unfortunately, Lucifer was successful in persuading one-third of the angels in Heaven to be unfaithful to God.[11] Thus, he and the angels who rebelled committed spiritual adultery.

8th Commandment—*You shall not steal.*

Lucifer "stole" a third of the angels, not to mention all the humans through earth's history who have rebelled against God and His law.[12]

---

[5] Isaiah 14:13
[6] Genesis 3:1–5
[7] Exodus 20:11
[8] Matthew 22:37
[9] Revelation 12:7
[10] Revelation 12:17
[11] Revelation 12:4
[12] Revelation 12:4

9th Commandment—*You shall not bear false witness.*

Lucifer became directly guilty of committing this sin when he misrepresented God's true character to the angels. Later on, he did the same thing with Eve in the Garden of Eden.[13]

10th Commandment—*You shall not covet.*

This may have been the very first sin Lucifer committed when he began desiring something that was not, and could not, ever be rightfully his—to be exalted above the throne of God.[14]

When we make a choice to follow God's commandments, we will find ourselves in a lifelong battle against our own sinful impulses and attitudes towards God and our fellow man. Many of Jesus's parables talk about the *natural consequences* that come from nurturing either positive or negative attitudes and behaviors.

One of Jesus's most famous talks on this topic was given during His Sermon on the Mount. In it, He expanded on the Ten Commandments by giving some real-world examples which clearly contrast heavenly and earthly values. These examples became known as the Beatitudes.[15]

As you read through the short summary below, please think about each value presented from the perspective of what kind of people *you* would like to live with forever in Heaven and on the New Earth. Ask yourself, What attitudes and behaviors would fit in with all the unfallen beings living throughout God's great universe?

- *Blessed are the poor in spirit . . .*

These are the people who **humbly** recognize their need for God. Humility is a direct antidote to pride and selfish independence.

- *Blessed are those who mourn . . .*

These people choose to **trust** God no matter what their circumstances may be. This provides comfort and hope.

- *Blessed are the meek . . .*

These are the people who are **gentle** with both words and actions.

---

[13] Genesis 3:1–5
[14] Isaiah 14:13–14
[15] Matthew 5:3–12

Meekness is a great safeguard for those who would be tempted to misuse power, be it physical, mental, financial, or social.

• *Blessed are those who hunger and thirst after righteousness . . .*

These people always **stand** for what is right, good, and true, even if taking a stand costs them fame, fortune, or freedom.

• *Blessed are the merciful . . .*

These are the people who are **sensitive** to the needs of others. They never laugh at or take pleasure from the pain, embarrassment, or misfortunes of others. They understand that extending mercy to others is a prerequisite to receiving forgiveness for yourself.

• *Blessed are the pure in heart . . .*

These people maintain a **pure**, childlike faith in the truth of God. Purity of purpose rejects all lies and deceptions, and all forms of physical, mental, emotional, or sexual abuse and coercion.

• *Blessed are the peacemakers . . .*

These are the people who make every effort to de-escalate and **reconcile** conflicts. Conflict resolution is at the heart of Christ's efforts to reconcile lost humans with each other and with God.

• *Blessed are they who are persecuted for righteousness sake . . .*

These people have made a **commitment** to stand for Christ and His righteousness even if their lives are on the line. This level of faithfulness is enabled by God's grace as needed.

In direct contrast to the values just presented, Paul described certain sins as being especially prevalent in the last days (our modern times) before Christ's second coming.[16] As you read Paul's description below, stop at each adjective or adverb and carefully consider whether or not they describe your behavior and attitudes and perhaps those of your family and friends as well.

> *"You should know this, Timothy, that in the last days there will be very difficult times. For people will love only themselves and their money. They will be boastful and proud, scoffing at God, disobedient to their parents, and ungrateful.*

---

[16] 2 Timothy 3:1–5

They will consider nothing sacred. They will be unloving and unforgiving; they will slander others and have no self-control. They will be cruel and hate what is good. They will betray their friends, be reckless, be puffed up with pride, and love pleasure rather than God. Some will even act religious, but they will reject the power that could make them godly. Stay away from people like that!"

People in virtually every nation, culture, business, school, and religion on earth today struggle with these very same negative attitudes and behaviors. Want proof? Check out any modern newspaper, magazine, or movie plot. Think about the story or situation presented and how our so-called "modern" social and political values have contributed to the acceptance of these attitudes and behaviors. Jesus even compared these behaviors with those that gave God reason to destroy the world with a flood and the cities of Sodom and Gomorrah with fire.[17]

So, how should we live our lives? Obviously, Jesus Christ is our ultimate role model. Think about the many stories from the New Testament illustrating how He met the needs of people from all walks of life, while living a humble, perfect life. Then, there are the many positive and negative examples of other people recorded in the Bible and in our history books. We need to learn from them, because if we don't, we will more than likely make the same mistakes and suffer the same consequences. History repeats itself.

Paul also talked about the struggles he had with sin in light of his own personal conversion experience. He described his own Christian walk as a sort of "tension" between knowing what is right but all too frequently doing what is wrong.[18] He found out that the key to making progress as an overcomer was to claim the promises of God for the enabling power of the Holy Spirit. He is the only One who can replace the desires of your sinful nature with the desires for a holy nature that match God's will for your life.[19]

---

[17] Luke 17:26–30
[18] Romans 7:15–25
[19] Galatians 5:16–17

Of course, this is where the devil changes tactics and tempts some churchgoers into thinking they are so *perfect* that they almost don't need a savior. Want proof? Check out what Christ Himself had to say about some of the church leadership in His day.[20] Pretty harsh words indeed! As Paul described, *they have a form of godliness* (on the outside) *but deny the power of God* (their conscience) *on the inside*.[21] This, of course, is the very definition of a hypocrite. The devil uses these people inside the church to spread discouragement and disillusionment among the spiritually young and those who are easily led astray from the Word of God.

So, it is vitally important for both the spiritually mature and the spiritually young to remember the following point. *If any of us could actually BE perfect in mind, body, and spirit, without any Divine assistance, Christ would never have had to endure a life of poverty and a cruel death on the cross for us.* Holy Scriptures state that all our righteousness is as "filthy rags" before the perfect character of God.[22] So, our need for a Savior is absolutely undeniable, no matter how spiritually mature we (or others) think we are. The question is, Do you humbly recognize your need?

Jesus stated, "If you love me, keep my commandments." (John 14:15) In other words, we are to make both the choice and the effort to live up to all the light we have. We are responsible for no more and no less. Jesus also said, "You shall love the Lord your God . . . and your fellow man as yourself." (Matthew 22:37–39) Virtually every story in the Bible about Jesus portrays compassionate, loving attitudes as the motivation for His many actions to benefit men, women, and children from every walk of life and in every circumstance.

So, what are some practical ways of growing our spiritual maturity here in the twenty-first century? The Holy Bible is filled with practical advice. In particular, the book of Proverbs comes to mind from the Old Testament. And in the New Testament, check out:

- *The characteristics of True Love*. I Corinthians 13:4–7 NLT

---

[20] Matthew 23:1–33 NLT

[21] 2 Timothy 3:5

[22] Isaiah 64:6

These verses are especially good for couples and families to read and talk about together from a modern translation of the Bible.

- *What not to do.* Colossians 3:5–9 NLT

These verses are especially good to read and think about when choosing or evaluating the friends you hang out with the most.

- *What to do.* Colossians 3:12–17 NLT

These verses will help you identify characteristics in people who will model and reinforce positive behaviors and attitudes.

- *What to think about.* Philippians 4:8–9 NLT, Colossians 3:1–2 NLT

These verses are talking about mental and emotional discipline.

It turns out that the *choice* to think positive thoughts is a necessary prerequisite to *produce* positive actions and attitudes.

When you are having a good day and life seems to be going along just fine, it is not too hard to think kind thoughts about others. But the challenge to our Christian witness comes when someone or something crosses our path and causes us distress of some kind. And in our modern, fast-paced life, short tempers and a lack of compassion for the point of view of others can make this a daily occurrence. This is why it is important to learn and practice positive anger management and conflict-resolution skills from childhood through adulthood.

In particular, it is important for the Christian to *practice* mental discipline. What do I mean by this? Scripture says that as a man (or woman) thinks, so is he (or she).[23] It is a psychological fact that if we *dwell* on themes such as violence, revenge, or forcing ourselves or our will on anyone else (even if it is *just* a movie or a video game), we will begin to unconsciously adopt this way of acting and reacting to situations, which cause us embarrassment, frustration, or what we perceive as injustice against us.

As examples of what I mean, think of the worst people in human history. Hitler, Stalin, and the like. Each of these individuals was born a sweet, innocent baby, as are all humans. But somewhere along the

---

[23] Proverbs 23:7 KJV

way, they each experienced a variety of situations or circumstances that caused them to *think* about a murderous response. Instead of controlling the rage within their minds through the choice to forgive, they chose to dwell on it until it resulted in actions, which consumed their lives and millions more.

The Christian has an unparalleled example in the life of Christ, as recorded in the Gospels. The Son of God quietly suffered every kind of humiliation, injustice, and inconvenience imaginable and yet maintained a dignified ability to forgive even those who crucified him on the cross. His exact words were, "Father, forgive them for they know not what they are doing." (Luke 23:34) Many people really don't know or care that their actions are bad. Others know it and embrace the idea fully. Only God can judge when they have crossed the line into unpardonable sin.

By the way, have you ever wondered what the unpardonable sin is? The definition is simple. It is any negative action or attitude for which you refuse the Holy Spirit's prompting to ask for (or extend to others) forgiveness. And what does repentance mean? It simply means you consciously choose to make a change away from sinful actions or attitudes, which the Holy Spirit convicts your conscience as being wrong or not beneficial to yourself or others.

Most legal systems recognize the difference between a criminal who feels remorse and is willing to change verses a *hardened* criminal who feels no remorse and is not willing to change. The first example might be rehabilitated and become a positive member of society again, but the other will not. This is also what the Bible means when it talks about a person who nurtures a *hardened* heart by willfully choosing to reject the conviction of the Holy Spirit to change his or her life to become a more humble, loving Christian.[24]

I believe *sanctification is the work of a lifetime.* This means that as our spiritual maturity grows, we will understand more and more of what it

---

[24] Hebrews 3:7–8 NLT

means to represent Christ by the way we live our lives. Naturally, this will be reflected by the way we treat others.

Micah 6:8 puts it this way. "He has showed you, O man, what is good; and what does the Lord require of you but to do justice, and to love kindness, and to walk humbly with your God?"

One very short (but sweet!) summary of how our positive attitudes and behaviors should be expressed is recorded in 1 Chronicles 4:10. This is often called the Prayer of Jabez.

"Oh, that you would bless me indeed, and enlarge my territory, that Your hand would be with me, and that You would keep me from evil, that I may not cause pain."

To summarize the concepts in this prayer, Jabez really wants the blessing of God on his life. He wants to be a good steward of all God blesses him with (time, talents, money, opportunities, etc.). He wants God to direct his life, to keep him from evil (by commission or omission). And finally, he wants God to help him avoid causing pain by his words, actions, or attitudes toward anybody or anything.

Does this sound like someone who would be safe to save? Would his or her attitudes and behavior be in harmony with the rest of the saved? Would the Holy Trinity, the angels, and all the rest of the unfallen inhabitants of the universe be comfortable living with such an individual for all eternity? More to the point, would YOU enjoy living next door to someone like this, both on this earth and in Heaven? For most of us, the answer would be a resounding YES!

PART V
MYTHS ABOUT HEAVEN

Our modern, media-driven society has propagated some myths about Heaven, which are clearly *not* correct, as revealed by what the Bible *does* state about Heaven. And, although I do *not* intend to be dogmatic about any of the *inferences* and *deductions* presented in this book, I *do* want to be biblically clear about dispelling some of the myths, which have troubled (and perhaps even terrified!) countless millions of young and old alike. Here are a few I'd like to address.

Myth #1: Halos, Clouds, Harps, and Wings

All we are going to do in Heaven is wear a halo and float around on top of the clouds while eternally strumming religious songs on a harp and flapping little wings sticking out of our back.

Unfortunately, some of our more popular TV cartoons present and reinforce this erroneous concept to our children at a very early age. I don't know about you, but spending all eternity acting out this scenario really doesn't sound too appealing to me. So, let's unpack the error behind this one bit by bit and see what we've really got.

Halos—While wearing halos of bright colors and different styles might be a welcome addition from time to time to our garments of light, there is no verse in the Bible that states we will be wearing one every minute for all eternity. However, it is true that God gave human beings the power to create, test, and revise on a nearly infinite scale. So, if wearing a halo is your thing, I look forward to seeing all the variety of designs you can come up with. And I just might see one I'd like to wear occasionally too!

Clouds—While I'm definitely looking forward to frequent opportunities to float around like a butterfly or glide around just over the treetops and mountains like a bird[1] or fly high and fast over the clouds like an airplane, there will undoubtedly be *many* other pursuits that will be just as interesting to explore and experience. However, I freely admit to being the type of person who would really enjoy sharing an occasional sunrise or sunset with my friends and loved ones while floating on top of the clouds. And a game of tag zipping over, around,

---

[1] Isaiah 40:31 KJV

or through the clouds during the daytime, or under the moon and stars in a clear, nighttime sky would be truly awesome. If this sounds like something you would enjoy too, I look forward to seeing you there. Oh, by the way, TAG—you're IT!

Harps—As far as the harp is concerned, I'm not really sure how this myth got started. God gave mankind enough intelligence to create many different kinds of musical instruments. Each can be used separately or in unison with other instruments and voices to create harmonious music of all types. This fact is clearly illustrated from numerous verses in the Bible about instrumental music.[2] However, if you really like playing a harp, I'm sure you'll get to play a beautiful, perfectly tuned version to your heart's content.

Wings—Finally, as for wings, I don't believe there are any verses in the Bible which would support this theory. Man was made to be a distinct order of being, which was different than the angels.[3] In particular, the Bible explicitly states that God made man in His own image and after His own likeness.[4] Since we humans were not originally created with wings, it stands to reason that our resurrected or translated forms will not have physical wings either.

Beyond this observation, I don't believe the angels actually *use* their wings to fly, as the birds are designed to do. The Bible does describe times when angels hovered in mid-air, and other times when they flew vast distances through space in answer to a prayer *while it was being spoken*.[5] I never saw any kind of bird fly like that.

I do believe we will have the ability to fly at will like the angels, either to get somewhere more quickly than walking would afford, or for the sheer joy and fun of flight. As for exactly *how* we will be able to do this, I suspect it will have something to do with how our translated bodies are able to interact with scientific principles, which operate in

---

[2] Psalm 150:1–6
[3] Psalm 8:5
[4] Genesis 1:26
[5] Luke 2:13–14, Daniel 9:21

dimensions of time, space, and matter we simply don't have sufficient mental IQ to understand at this time. But no matter how it is done, I'm sure it will be a lot of fun to experience the joy of flight like the angels do!

Myth #2: Singing, Singing, and MORE Singing!

All we are going to do forever and ever is sing praises to God in a choir full of angels, sitting around His throne room in Heaven.

The Book of Revelation repeatedly says this is what some of the *angels* were made for.[1] But it does not say this is what *we* were made for. Nor does it imply that this is all we will do in Heaven.

The Bible says that man was created in the image of God to give glory to his Creator.[2] God can be glorified by the life of a human being in many different ways. This concept was illustrated by the life of Jesus Christ while He was here on this earth. In fact, human beings have always been blessed with a multitude of talents, skills, and intelligences when it comes to expressing praise, honor, and glory to their Creator.

While the singing of praises to God will undoubtedly be done on a frequent basis, both spontaneously and as planned events, many verses in the Bible make it clear that everything else we do will also be done to the glory of God.[3] It is the *attitude of gratitude* which gives God constant praise in the life of a committed Christian, whether living on this present earth, up in Heaven, or on the New Earth. This is what it means to "walk and talk" with God.

---

[1] Revelation 5:11–12, Revelation 7:11–12
[2] Genesis 1:26, Isaiah 43:7
[3] Hebrews 13:15

Myth #3: Fire Insurance— a HOT Topic!

I need to be saved just so I won't burn in hell forever.

On the surface, being saved for this reason appears to be nothing more than "fire insurance." You definitely don't want to go to Hell, but you really aren't sure Heaven would be a fun place to live either. The real danger with this view is the assumption that God is a harsh and mean-spirited being, instead of someone to feel safe, accepted, and loved by. This distortion of God's true character is exactly what the devil wants you to believe about Him.

Proverbs 1:7 does state that, "The fear of the Lord is the beginning of all wisdom." However, a more accurate translation would substitute the words *awe* and *respect* for the word *fear* to clarify the original intent of the text. Clearly, we serve an awesome God.

But He is also the same God who showed such great compassion and love for us that He sent His beloved son to pay the penalty of sin for all those who would accept and respond to His sacrifice.[1] Jesus Christ expressly represented His Father's true character by living a life of humility, gentleness, and love.[2] His words and actions have inspired countless men, women, and children to commit their lives to Him. And finally, His sacrifice for our sins has provided the entire universe with a very sharp contrast between the Father's true character and Satan's false accusations and lies.

Now, let's straighten out this idea of "once saved, always saved" once and for all. The Bible makes it clear we must initially *believe* in the Lord Jesus Christ to be saved.[3] But our obligation to *respond* to

---

[1] Romans 5:8
[2] John 14:7–11
[3] John 3:16

the convictions of the Holy Spirit and *grow* the relationship spiritually during our entire lifetime does not stop there.[4] As an example, let me point to Lucifer, also known as the devil and Satan.

Say what you will about the devil, but one thing he is definitely *not* is an atheist. Satan knows all too well that Jesus Christ really exists and that He was the Creator of our world and countless others. Satan also knows Jesus humbled Himself to be born on this earth as a very real, flesh-and-blood, human baby boy.

In spite of all the trials and temptations he and his fellow demons hurled at Jesus day and night, they all know He lived a perfect life. They also instigated a truly cruel death on the cross, thinking that would finish Him off for good. Then, they were utterly powerless to stop Jesus from being physically raised from the dead, thus sealing their eventual eternal doom.

So, it would be technically correct to say the devil and his host of fellow demons fully *believe* Jesus Christ exists and is who He claims to be. However, none of them will be saved in spite of this knowledge. The reason has to do with their lack of a positive response to the truth about God's character. In short, it was their own choice to reject Jesus Christ as the rightful King of all He has created, not their belief in Him, which will result in their ultimate and complete destruction in the purifying fires of hell.[5]

True salvation means continually growing in your spiritual knowledge, values, and experiential relationship with God. This growing spiritual maturity will be naturally reflected by a humble attitude, a forgiving spirit, and a positive relationship with your fellow man. This is precisely why Jesus Christ clearly stated, "If you love me, you will want to obey my commandments."[6]

The Ten Commandments outline our duty to God and to each

---

[4] 1 Corinthians 14:20 NLT, 2 Peter 3:18 NLT
[5] Ezekiel 28:18 NLT, Malachi 4:1 NLT
[6] John 14:15 NLT

other. The Beatitudes[7] and many other verses in the Bible refine the framework of attitudes and behaviors established by the Ten Commandments. So, if your words, actions, and values[8] reflect this kind of thinking, then Heaven will be the kind of place where you will feel completely comfortable and totally satisfied for all eternity.

There, you will feel a vibrant sense of happiness, freedom, and belonging you can scarcely imagine in this life. In turn, it will be the most natural thing imaginable to praise God for saving you from the irreconcilable consequences of your own sins—an eternal separation from God, which is the ultimate definition of hell.

---

[7] Matthew 5:3–11
[8] 1 Corinthians 13:4–7

Myth #4: A Topic of Concern to All—Oh NO!

The desire for sex is inherently bad and immoral, so that is why there won't be any sex or marriage in Heaven.

Ask any teenager what worries him or her the most about living in Heaven, and the feared lack of sexual intimacy and marriage will always be at the very top of the list. This is because it is a perfectly natural thing for young people (and many older people as well!) to have an intense desire to enjoy an intimate, loving relationship with a spouse for life. Many of us firmly believe this kind of marital relationship can be a foretaste of Heaven itself. And so, it is extremely hard for most people to imagine being totally happy and content forever without being able to share a close, intimate, sexual relationship with a spouse, within the covenant of marriage.

Unfortunately, a full range of erroneous concepts about sex, marriage, and Heaven have been recorded by both secular and religious historians. For example, some world religions suggest each man will have many virgin wives in Heaven, regardless of their marital status on this earth.[1] So, if all the saved men in Heaven are only married to virgins, then exactly who will all their previously married, saved mothers, wives, sisters, and daughters live with? Other religions have put forth the idea of worshiping their ancestors[2] or being reincarnated as an animal or as some other human being, all of which entirely sidesteps the promise of Heaven and a New Earth.

On the other end of the spectrum, some ultra-conservative church leaders have valiantly tried to label any notion of a passionate relationship between a man and a woman as being immoral, carnal,

---

[1] https://www.zwemercenter.com/muslim-views-of-heaven/
[2] https://www.joincake.com/blog/ancestor-worship/

and sinful.³ Therefore, they believe this kind of relationship could not possibly be a part of God's plan for the saved in Heaven. It is no wonder at all why so many young people have left the Christian church over the seriously dysfunctional concepts presented to them about love, sex, and marriage, especially as these ideas relate to living eternally with a God who says He IS love.⁴

Once young people leave the church, many of them begin to experiment with the idea of just living together. Since living together implies a physically intimate relationship *without* a lifelong commitment, God cannot bless such a relationship. In fact, this kind of relationship is extremely dangerous to both parties. Sexually transmitted diseases, physical, mental, emotional, spiritual, and financial abuse and/or neglect, and unstable homes for any resulting children are just some of the negatives that bring about terrible, far-reaching consequences on all individuals involved.

On the other hand, a couple can have a beautiful church wedding and a framed certificate of marriage on the bedroom wall and *still* lack a lifetime commitment to each other's well-being and happiness. Sadly, the divorce statistics for couples married inside the church nearly match those for couples married elsewhere.⁵ And the consequences are even more devastating because of the negative witness of irreconcilable differences between two people who claim to be Christians.

So, what is the answer? The key is found in the first part of the last sentence of the typical pronouncement of marriage: **"What God has joined together,** let no man put apart." The couple must invite God to be the One who unites them in the covenant of holy matrimony. This decision must be mutually agreed upon by the couple *before* the wedding. And it must be mutually acted upon by the couple *after* the

---

³ https://www.desiringgod.org/messages/christian-hedonists-or-religious-prudes-the-puritans-on-sex

⁴ 1 John 4:8 KJV

⁵ https://www.news24.com/news24/xArchive/Voices/more-christians-divorce-than-non-believers-according-to-statistics-20180719

wedding so their relationship can gradually mature to what God designed marriage to be—a foretaste of Heaven. This is just one of many reasons why the Bible states, "Do not be unequally yoked together with unbelievers."[6]

Of course, once a couple agrees to marry each other, then they should jointly share this decision with their mutual families and friends in a carefully planned social occasion to celebrate the engagement, betrothal, or legal marriage. However, all parties must remember that the most important factor to God is not how chronologically old, educated, or economically stable the couple is, as important as these factors are today. What matters far more is a seriously mature commitment of both husband and wife to love, honor, and cherish each other for as long as they both shall live. But have you ever wondered why marriage vows come with one very significant stipulation? They only apply until one partner dies.

One of the most difficult issues a married couple will ever face is what happens when one partner dies before the other. For most of earth's history, the high mortality rates for young women in childbirth and for young men at war added to the significant illness and injury rates of a normal life, which resulted in a fair probability of losing your mate early in the typical marriage.

So, do we condemn these countless millions of young widows and widowers to live the rest of their lives without the benefits of a loving spouse or a stable, two-parent home for their children, just because they must worry about whom they will be married to in Heaven if they remarry here on earth? God forbid! I firmly believe this dilemma is *exactly* what Jesus was thinking about when He gave His famous answer to the Sadducees who tried to trap Him with a question about the resurrection, disguised within a seemingly unanswerable question about marriage in Heaven.[7] But before we discuss His answer, let me clarify several other things.

---

[6] 2 Corinthians 6:14
[7] Mark 12:18–25

In spite of Satan's continuous efforts to distort and pervert sex and marriage, the Bible pictures the physically intimate union of one man and one woman within the lifetime commitment of marriage as being designed and ordained by God for their supreme benefit. Therefore, what He created and blessed over 6,000 years ago in the Garden of Eden remains completely good for us today.[8] Remember, the Bible says that our God doesn't change His mind about things He states unequivocally like this.[9]

But would marriage (as we know it) be beneficial to our life in Heaven or on the New Earth? Based on God's original design for Adam and Eve, I believe resurrected and translated human beings will have the very same needs and desires as they do now. The fact that Jesus was resurrected with a fully human, touchable body, complete with the need to eat, further reinforces this concept.[10]

I also firmly believe God's original purposes for mankind will *eventually* be fully restored. Those original purposes definitely included close, intimate family units, all praising His name for life, liberty, and love. So, I think the real question is not *if*, but *when* will each of our individual needs for that kind of companionship be addressed? Could it happen at some point during the Millennium, or after the New Earth is re-created? It is definitely possible.

Without a doubt, we serve a God who is omnipotently creative. He is also the Master Designer, after all. So, I'm absolutely certain He can solve the dilemma of how to meet our built-in needs for intimate companionship and love within a human family unit in a multitude of ways. I'm also equally certain that He will specifically tailor a solution for each one of the saved, which will be completely satisfying to us beyond our wildest imagination. Psalms 16:11 assures us, "In your presence is fullness of joy, and at your right hand are pleasures forevermore."

To think that God would not make provision for meeting the very

---

[8] Genesis 2:18–24 NLT, Matthew 19:4–6 NLT
[9] Malachi 3:6
[10] Luke 24:39–43, 1 Corinthians 15:3–8

needs He personally created within each of us would be the same thing as suggesting He somehow made a *big mistake* in creating men and women with a natural desire to have a close, intimate bond with a spouse in the first place. We will further examine this idea in the next section to see if we can deduce the real truth.

Myth #5: BIG Oops— God Made a Mistake!

When God gave men and women the desire and ability to passionately enjoy sex and procreation, He made a BIG mistake!

Genesis 2:18 clearly records God the Father specifically stating it was *not good for the man to be alone*. It is important to note God said this *before* He created the first woman. But did God create another male for Adam, just so he wouldn't be all alone? No! Did He create an angel to be Adam's earthly companion? No!

God created a female human being specifically designed to be desired by Adam as his most intimate companion.[1] He also created Eve to desire Adam as her most intimate companion too. Then, He united the couple in marriage and commanded them to be fruitful and multiply.[2] Finally, He blessed them and pronounced His supreme satisfaction with everything He had done.[3]

Therefore, it would be entirely correct to say that God Himself invented and blessed sexual activity *within the boundaries of a marriage commitment*. God's purpose for sexual activity was to enhance the unity the couple would feel together as well as to provide for the procreation of children. To accomplish this, He deliberately designed the chemistry of the human body and brain to fully enjoy having a passionate relationship with a spouse, and to love any resulting children. They, in turn, have a built-in need for a mom and dad, all living together as an intact family unit.

In this present life, the very highest levels of stress are generated when a happily married couple experiences the death or involuntary

---

[1] Genesis 2:21–23 KJV
[2] Genesis 1:28 KJV
[3] Genesis 1:31 KJV

separation of a spouse or a child. So, it stands to reason that one of the chief attractions of Heaven for them would be God's absolute and unequivocal promise stating there will be no more heartache, tears, or pain from separation experienced ever again.[4] Without a doubt, if both happily married spouses are saved, then they will most certainly want to continue living together in the state of holy matrimony, along with their saved children, as a completely intact family unit. No separate mansions for them!

But just suppose God said something like this on resurrection morning: *"Okay, all you couples who were happily married, you will need to choose your own separate mansions when we get to Heaven. Your sons and daughters will need to split up too. And all you teenagers and adults who never got married, well, you are just plain out of luck now. As for all the countless babies who died before being born, and those children who died while growing up, you will be raised by angels instead of having your own two-parent human family. And by the way, you can also forget about ever getting married when you do grow up and want a family of your own."* Now wouldn't this be a cruel twist to the idea of eternal happiness?

To think God is going to hand divorce papers to all the happily married saved couples on resurrection morning, then tell each mom and dad and their children, and all their other relatives that they will all have to live in separate mansions immediately upon arrival to the New Jerusalem would be completely ludicrous. But more to the point, these actions would also be completely out of character for a God who originally invented both marriage and the family unit. This is because He specifically pronounced them "very good," and then declared throughout Scripture that He does not change His word—ever.[5]

I'm certain Satan would like for us to think God made a big mistake in giving mankind the ability to procreate and to actually enjoy the process. And without a doubt, Satan has capitalized on the destructive nature of sexual abuse, infidelity, and divorce to destroy many families.

---

[4] Revelation 21:4 KJV
[5] Malachi 3:6 KJV

These terrible vices are second only to the atrocities and mass casualties of all-out war between nations as the greatest causes of human misery and suffering down through recorded history.

But, since God never makes mistakes, then perhaps we will be reincarnated as something not fully human. Maybe we will actually BE angels. Could this be the reason some people think we will not need, or even want a close sexual union in Heaven, even if our earthly spouse is saved? Let's examine these possibilities next.

Myth #6: No Physical Bodies

Since we won't have physical bodies when we are resurrected, we won't have any desires for sex or a close, intimate family.

Some people actually believe we won't have physical bodies in Heaven. We will just be ethereal spirits sitting around on clouds, strumming our harps for all eternity. But if this were true, then why was Jesus resurrected in human form as a man, with a touchable, physical body, complete with the need to eat?[1]

And yet, He was also able to appear, disappear, transport himself unseen, and reappear to many hundreds of eye-witnesses.[2] He also ascended bodily into the atmosphere without any visible means of lift, and He was able to travel through space to Heaven without artificial means, just like the angels.[3] So, Jesus conclusively demonstrated that those who are resurrected and translated will have real, genuine human bodies, with the added benefit of sharing *some* of the characteristic abilities of the angels. But it is important to remember that we won't actually BE angels, because we will still possess our own human male and female physical, mental, and emotional characteristics completely intact.

Jesus was definitely not resurrected as some wisp of spiritual vapor, nor did His spirit ascend to Heaven while He was physically lying dead in the tomb. He stated as much while talking with Mary Magdalene, when she found His tomb empty.[4] Finally, it is His *empty* tomb which provides the most compelling evidence for the promise of a physical resurrection and an eternal life.[5] Without that *empty* tomb, absolutely no discussion of heaven would matter because it would be forever out of reach to you and me!

---

[1] Luke 24:36–43
[2] Luke 24:30–31, 1 Corinthians 15:3–8 NLT
[3] Luke 24:51
[4] John 20:16–17
[5] John 20:1–9

PART VI
TROUBLING ANSWER TO A TRICK QUESTION

What Jesus Said and Why

Now that we have a better understanding about some of the more common myths our modern society perpetuates about Heaven, let's take a look at what disturbs many people the most about this topic. And that has to do with how to reconcile what God the Father said about marriage, as opposed to what Jesus Christ said about marriage at the resurrection. Perhaps, if we consider the audience each was speaking to, it will give us a better contextual background to understand these seemingly irreconcilable statements.

God the Father was speaking to Adam and Eve and all their expected posterity, *before* sin entered the picture. Based on His statement, as recorded by Moses in the Book of Genesis, God's *original purpose* was for Adam and Eve to experience the joy and happiness of marriage and a family unit *for all eternity*. This blessing definitely included a sexual union between the husband and wife.[1]

God the Son was speaking to a group of Sadducees, in front of a multitude of people who probably represented every possible combination of single, married, widowed, divorced, homosexual, polygamous, and abused relationship imaginable. Based on His statement, as recorded by Matthew and Mark, no one will be getting married on resurrection morning.[2] Well, that is for sure and certain, as we shall soon see!

Some commentators have applied an extended meaning to these passages by stating there will be no marriage (at least as we commonly understand it) in Heaven or on the New Earth *after* resurrection morning either. Although I have not found any direct scriptural support for this belief, we must keep an open mind about this possibility without fearing a negative consequence. This is because we serve a God of Love who has promised that *every* aspect of Heaven will satisfy us beyond anything we can imagine.

---

[1] Genesis 1:28, Genesis 2:21–24
[2] Matthew 22:29–30, Mark 12:24–25

Psalm 16:11 says, "In your presence is fullness of joy, and at your right hand are pleasures forevermore." Therefore, we must not allow ourselves to think God is limited by our present experience or our puny imagination when it comes to meeting the physical, emotional, and sexual needs He created within each of us.

So, with this background of information, we will now look more closely at exactly what Jesus said in the New Testament on the topic. Next, we will employ the same *deductive* and *inferential* reasoning skills we've been developing all along in this book to explore the possible context of *why* He said what He did. Finally, we will consider the different perspectives all those multiple individuals in His audience may have had on this topic.

The hypothetical scenario posed by the Sadducees to Jesus in front of the crowd involved a woman who was consecutively married to seven brothers, each of whom died without leaving any children to provide for her. The question they posed to Jesus was, "Whose wife would she be in Heaven?"[3]

Matthew 22:29–30 and Mark 12:24–25 quote Jesus's response, as follows: "You are mistaken, not knowing the Scriptures nor the power of God. For when the dead rise, they neither marry nor are given in marriage, but are like the angels in Heaven."

Now, let's unpack exactly what Jesus is saying here.

- **You are mistaken, not knowing the Scriptures . . .**

Jesus begins by pointing out the Sadducees error in not knowing what the Scriptures actually say about the resurrection. Their ignorance on this subject was further compounded by the fact that they didn't acknowledge any Scripture beyond the first five books of the Old Testament, which are collectively called the Pentateuch.

- **. . . nor the power of God.**

The Sadducees did not believe in the power of God to resurrect the dead because they didn't see a direct reference to this in the Pentateuch.

---

[3] Matthew 22:23–28, Mark 12:18–23

This is the part of the question they were most interested in and where they thought they could trap Jesus in His answer.

- **For when the dead rise . . .**

The dead will rise on resurrection morning at the second coming.

- **. . . they neither marry nor are given in marriage . . .**

Now, let's pause here for a moment and picture some of the events Scripture says will be happening on resurrection morning.

First, the righteous dead will be getting resurrected and reunited in the air with their saved parents, spouses, children, extended family members, and friends.[4] Next, the righteous living will be getting translated and reunited with all their saved loved ones and friends as part of the glorious resurrection scene.[5] The unrighteous living will be getting destroyed.[6] And the earth, the oceans, and the atmosphere will be convulsing with all the forces of nature gone completely wild.[7] Given this scenario, I am quite certain NO man or woman will be thinking about a wedding once these worldwide events get fully started on resurrection morning.

- **. . . but are like the angels in Heaven.**

Again, it is important to emphasize Jesus never said we would actually *become* angels. The Bible says we were initially created to be a little lower than the angels.[8] But it is important to remember it never said we were to stay at that level of development.

So, Jesus is telling us we will finally share at least *some* of the angel's characteristic abilities right away, on resurrection morning. These abilities will enable the translated humans to safely travel the distance through time and space between our world and the New Jerusalem in Heaven just *as* the angels do. But it does not mean we will lose our human male or female characteristics and actually become angels. Jesus

---

[4] 1 Thessalonians 4:16
[5] 1 Thessalonians 4:17
[6] Matthew 13:49 and Revelation 6:14–17
[7] 2 Peter 3:10–13
[8] Hebrews 2:7

conclusively demonstrated this fact when He was resurrected in human form as a man, not as an angel.[9]

Finally, Jesus nails any doubt about His position on whether or not there will actually BE a resurrection. He refers the Sadducees to a portion of the Pentateuch that talks about God's power to resurrect the dead. *He is the God of the living, not the dead.*[10]

Now, let's consider the most likely reason why Jesus worded His answer the way He did. First of all, I don't believe Jesus ever intended for His statement to cause concern to those who were happily married or distress to those who were still single. In fact, I believe His intention was to give scriptural support to the countless millions of men and women down through history who would struggle with whether or not to remarry when a beloved mate died. He wanted to set them free from worrying about the effect a remarriage on earth might have on whom they would be living with in Heaven.

To give some additional background on where I'm going with this, let's remember that before the advent of modern medicine, it was a common thing to lose one's mate to a wide variety of causes. Young men frequently died in warfare. Young women frequently died in childbirth. And everyone from the very young to the very old were susceptible to a wide variety of fatal illnesses, diseases, and accidents. So, it was not uncommon for the average person to have a valid need to marry more than once during their lifetime.

The modern twentieth-century concept of childhood lasting through the first eighteen years of life, followed by a life expectancy of some sixty or more years of adulthood, was not very common in Jesus's time. By some estimates, the *average* lifespan in those times was only around forty-four years![11] This helps to explain many cultural norms, which might be viewed as immoral or illegal in most countries today. Children were *expected* by their parents, extended family, and

---

[9] Luke 24:36–43

[10] Exodus 3:6 KJV

[11] https://earlychurchhistory.org/daily–life/longevity–in–the–ancient–world/

What Jesus Said and Why / 93

governmental authorities to assume adult responsibilities at a very early age.

For example, the average chronological age which a young boy might be considered an adult was usually from fourteen to seventeen.[12] Boys of this age were often drafted into military service, apprenticed to a craftsman, or put to work in the mines or fields or on state-sponsored construction projects. Girls between twelve to fourteen years of age were often contracted out as house servants or married off and expected to be ready to run a household and raise children of their own.[13]

To illustrate this point further, Luke 1:30 explicitly states that, "Mary found favor with God" as He personally selected her to be the mother of Jesus Christ. Yet, given the social norms of her time, there is a very high probability she was no older than a mid-teen.[14] So, it should be quite apparent that the mental, emotional, and spiritual maturity and stability of an individual are far more important to God than mere chronological age. Mary's consent is recorded in Luke 1:38 as follows: "Behold the handmaid of the Lord; be it unto me according to thy word." Maturity at its finest.

As Mary's betrothed, Joseph is understood to have been considerably older than she was. In fact, Joseph may have been a widower with children of his own.[15] Yet he was definitely not a selfish, perverted old man. To the contrary, Matthew 1:19 states, "Joseph was a just man."

In fact, God directly intervened when Joseph was preparing to break his engagement to Mary over what appeared to be her unfaithfulness to him during their engagement, resulting in an unexpected pregnancy.[16] So, it is evident God affirmed Mary's choice of Joseph to be her husband despite their age difference, or maybe even because of

---

[12] Philip King and Lawrence Stager, *Life in Biblical Israel*, Westminster John Knox Press, Louisville, KY, 2001, p 37

[13] Merrill C. Tenney, Editor, *The Zondervan Pictorial Encyclopedia of the Bible*, Regency Reference Library, Grand Rapids, MI, 1976, Vol. 4, p.96.

[14] https://spiritandtruthonline.org/mary-a-teenage-bride-and-mother/

[15] Matthew 13:55–56

[16] Matthew 1:20–25 KJV

it! Together, they were given the awesome responsibility of raising and schooling Jesus Christ through His early years on this earth. Apparently, they made quite a team!

Now, let's make the question of marriage in Heaven relevant here. Suppose Joseph is saved, Mary is saved, and Joseph's previous wife is saved. They meet up in Heaven and all three are wondering whom they will share their mansions with. Who is Jesus going to give Joseph's previous wife to? And who will Jesus give His mother Mary to live with? To further compound the situation, let's suppose that Joseph is *not* saved. Now who will Jesus give Mary and Joseph's previous wife to live with for all eternity?

Can you imagine the pandemonium that would break out on resurrection morning if God DIDN'T raise or translate us like the angels? *"What are you doing with my wife?" "Get your hands off my husband!"* Multiply these scenarios by all the hundreds of millions of saved individuals over the last 6,000 years who have experienced the loss of a spouse and remarried someone they learned to love differently, equally, or maybe even more than their previous spouse.

Now, are you beginning to see just how complicated things could rapidly get with these issues? Obviously, someone is going to get their feelings severely hurt when subsequent marriage partners are discovered or rejected! But doesn't the Bible also say there will be no more tears or heartache in Heaven about *any* issue?[17] So, how do we get around all the potential "issues," which would definitely be caused by the scenarios presented above on resurrection morning?

Emotional stress over questions like this becomes a very real matter for Christians who have had to grapple with the death of a beloved spouse. I firmly believe Jesus knew all of this and wanted to set them at liberty to remarry without this worry. So, from this perspective, it makes perfect sense to raise or translate us initially "*like* or *as* the angels" regarding how we relate to each other.

---

[17] Isaiah 65:17 KJV, Revelation 21:4

But the Scriptures say nothing about how long our relationships with other humans will remain this way. Could this be a temporary condition until God, in His infinite wisdom, gets all family relationships sorted out to everyone's complete satisfaction? I don't know. But the Bible is clear about God's ultimate intention to restore mankind to where he was before sin entered the picture.[18]

Had Adam and Eve not fallen into sin, they would have continued to enjoy the passionate bonding experience of sexual union together for all eternity. Why else would God purposefully design and make all the pleasure sensors in Adam and Eve's reproductive organs? They were certainly not necessary just for the procreation of our species, as is clearly demonstrated by animal reproduction.

Some might ask what would have happened to the sexual experience if Adam and Eve had NOT fallen into sin? If they and all their descendants lived forever and continued to reproduce, sooner or later, the entire planet would be in danger of overpopulation. If this had happened, would God suddenly declare, *"Okay, you've had your fun. Now it is all over."* I don't think so.

To take this thought to a whole new level, do you really think Adam and Eve and all their descendants would have been limited to living just on this earth? There are countless other inhabited worlds in God's great universe.[19] And since God is constantly creating, who is to say He wouldn't create "Earth 2" for us populate?

The point is, God originally designed the sexual union between husband and wife to be one of the most pleasurable bonding experiences we can possibly know. In fact, the Bible uses the words *know* and *knew* to describe this union.[20] And then, God pronounced total satisfaction with His handiwork.[21] So, why would He suddenly reverse course and say we will never have the intense personal pleasure of *knowing* a beloved spouse again?[22]

[18] Acts 3:21
[19] Job 38:7
[20] Genesis 4:1
[21] Genesis 1:31
[22] Malachi 3:6

That makes no sense, especially if you consider what a difference it makes to most of us to share the beauty of God's creation with a beloved mate. Something as simple as a sunrise or sunset is made so much more enjoyable when shared with someone we love. Without a doubt, the pleasures of living in a mansion in heaven would be greatly diminished without the love, affection, and companionship of a beloved mate, children, and extended family to share it with.

Now, for most of this chapter, we've been talking about happily married couples. This audience would include the following two categories of people with positive marital experiences:

• Those who have been *happily married to one spouse* during their entire married lifetime and are definitely looking forward to sharing all the beauty and joy of eternity with that same spouse.

• Those who have been *happily married several times*, due to the death of a previous spouse, but have no idea which one they would want to spend all eternity living with in Heaven.

Next, we will briefly explore some other audiences which may have very different expectations regarding marriage, including:

• Those who have *never been married*, but can't imagine being happy in this life or in Heaven without sharing an intimate relationship with a companion of the opposite sex.

• Those who have *never been married*, and due to a variety of reasons (abuse, neglect, etc.), don't want to think about being married in this life or in the next.

• Those who have been *unhappily married to one or more spouses* and really don't want to think about being married to anyone ever again, on this earth or in Heaven.

It should be obvious that each of these audiences would have a somewhat different reaction to the possibility of marriage in Heaven. Some might be glad, some might be mad, some might be sad, and some might not want to think about this subject at all.

Jesus knew all this when he gave His famous answer to the Sadducees. But again, I believe He was primarily addressing the needs of those who would lose a beloved spouse because they would be in the greatest majority throughout most of history. They would also be the ones with the most need to re-marry for the sake of their children and (sometimes) for their own sheer survival in the mostly male-dominated cultures throughout earth's history.

But least we forget, God did not create another man for Adam or give him an angel for companionship. Instead, He carefully made a fantastically beautiful, incredibly intelligent, wonderfully spirited female helpmate who He knew Adam would naturally love, respect, and enjoy as his wife for all eternity.

From Eve's point of view, she must have thought Adam was created specially to delight her, which in fact he was! Then God pronounced their union as "very good!" So, what makes any of us think God can't either create the right person for us or bring us into contact with the right saved person to share and enjoy all the beauty and wonder of Heaven with for all eternity?

Of course, time itself will have a completely new meaning in Heaven as well. The expenditure of time there will no longer seem like the sacrifice it actually is here in this present life. This is a natural byproduct of living in a place where time will no longer dictate everything that happens in our lives, like it does here.

So, no matter how long it takes before God addresses the question of intimate companionship personally for each one of the saved, I truly don't believe any of us will suffer the anxiety of wondering if we will be blessed with a family of our very own to share and fully enjoy all the beauty and wonder of Heaven for all eternity.

What Jesus Didn't Say and Why

Now, let's take a look at what Jesus did *not* say about marriage. Although He is quoted in the Bible as saying there would be no marriage or giving in marriage *at the resurrection*, He didn't say anything at all about how we would relate to one another in Heaven or on the New Earth. Could it be, during our thousand-year millennium in Heaven, we will all mutually agree upon who we really want to live with in a close, intimate family unit? Or perhaps God, in His infinite wisdom, will decide this question for us.

What about all those individuals who will be in Heaven that were never married on earth? This would also include all the countless babies and young children who never had a chance to grow up and be married in this life to begin with. Beyond this question is precisely *who* is going to raise all those human babies and children in Heaven? Certainly not the angels! God wired human children to want and need a loving human mother and father, all living together in the same home as a close, intimate family unit. Where does this fit with the notion of not having any married couples or families at all in Heaven?

And consider this for a moment. Do you think any of us, married or single, would actually enjoy rattling around in our heavenly mansion all alone, without any mate, children, or close family to hug, kiss, caress, or hold hands with? And no, I don't believe for one second that our heavenly mansions will be constructed like dormitories for one sex or another. God *never* intended for men, women, and children to live segregated apart from a homogeneous family unit. Heaven will definitely NOT be an eternal singles club!

Some would argue that in Heaven, we will all be close family and share at least brotherly love. While this is probably true, God did *not* make Adam and Eve to be brother and sister. Nor did He make them to be just best friends, although I would strongly recommend that every husband and wife actually BE each other's best friend, both before *and* after the wedding. No friends, relatives, or children should ever come between a husband and a wife.

God deliberately designed Adam and Eve to be an intimately loving, thoroughly affectionate couple, *before* sin entered the picture. So, if the New Earth is to be restored to its original state of sinless perfection, it stands to reason that *so will we*! The Bible says we were originally created a little lower than the angels.[1] But we also had the power to procreate the human race and to eventually mature into sons and daughters of God, which may be a higher state of existence than even the angels themselves.

And yet, there is still the question of precisely what Jesus meant when he added that we shall "be as the angels in heaven." Does anyone here on earth know how the angels are made? Sometimes, artists and authors project our understanding of male or female characteristics onto angels as they try to picture or describe human encounters with them. But we have no real evidence of what physical properties the angels of God have, nor do we know how they relate to each other on personal or intimate levels. Are they male, female, unisex, or no sex at all? If you can answer these questions, you've got a lot more insight than I have!

I believe a better way of understanding the concept of how we will be *like* the angels would be to think of some of the qualities and characteristics we may share with them, without actually *being* angels. For instance, I have already mentioned clothing of light, the ability to transport oneself by many different methods, the ability to walk and talk with each member of the Trinity, etc. *We must also acknowledge the distinct possibility that there may be other dimensions and forms of physical love and companionship we simply are not able to comprehend right now.* To illustrate this idea, let's carefully consider these following two scenarios.

---

[1] Psalm 8:5

The Bible says the lowly ant is actually quite a wise creature.[2] And yet, you would not be able to explain the beauty of a sunset, how it feels to fall in love, or how to construct a nuclear submarine to an ant, because it does not have the intellect or frame of reference to understand what you are saying. The same could also be said of a human baby. However, *the crucial difference is that human babies can grow up and develop the intellectual capacity to fully understand and experience what you are talking about.*

The three-year-old who is completely fixated on a beautiful, red pedal car simply can't comprehend your description of the enjoyment available from driving a beautiful, red sports car sitting just out of view on the other side of a curtain. But when that same three-year-old is sixteen, he or she will fully understand the context of how much more enjoyable and desirable the sport car is as compared to the pedal car. The same will hold true for the saved.

Although I've done my best to give you some idea of what could be waiting on the other side of the "veil of eternity," none of us really has the intellectual development yet to fully understand what God has prepared for us to inherit. This is why John the Revelator and others who were given a quick peak all reported that what they saw was beyond their ability to describe. But with all of eternity at our disposal, plus the incredible potential of intellectual and physical qualities, which *never* get tired, bored, or overloaded, only God knows for sure what we can develop and ultimately experience in the way of intimate personal relationships.

Again, we must remember that God has omnipotent creativity and creative omnipotence. He can create anything out of nothing, He can resurrect anything out of nothing, and He can re-create anything He chooses for our ultimate happiness and satisfaction. So, it seems to be well within the realm of our present reasoning skills to believe God can provide each of us with the one companion who is best suited for us,

---

[2] Proverbs 6:6

at exactly the right time to do so, just like He did for Adam and Eve and many others in the Bible.

In the meantime, let us choose to trust Him to provide an immensely satisfying solution that *no one*, young or old, married or unmarried here on this earth needs to fear as being anything less than spectacularly enjoyable in every possible way!

Finally, let us rest this question by simply choosing to *trust* Him to provide the very best possible answer to our built-in need for a close, intimate family unit. I have absolutely no doubt that we will join together with all the saved in praising His name for a solution far beyond anything we could have *ever* imagined here on this old earth. Who could possibly be better to trust our eternal love life with than a God who states He IS love?

PART VII
THE MOST IMPORTANT THING IN THIS BOOK

HAPPY MOMENTS,
Praise God.
DIFFICULT MOMENTS,
Seek God.
QUIET MOMENTS,
Worship God.
PAINFUL MOMENTS,
Trust God.
EVERY MOMENT,
Thank God.

Trust in the Lord with All Your Heart

In our modern age of evolutionary scientific thought, some say God has no place in our lives. Some people even say God does not exist. "The fool has said in his heart that there is no God." (Psalm 14:1) None of us wants to admit to being a fool! Even the devil and his demons aren't atheists. They all know very well that God exists! Why else do you think they have worked so hard to deceive so many people throughout history into thinking God either doesn't exist or doesn't matter on a personal level?

Others think that if He does exist, He doesn't care enough about the human condition of suffering, sickness, and death to do anything meaningful about it. The devil and his demons love this kind of misguided thinking. Virtually every recorded event in Christ's life should be enough to counter this notion, not to mention the ministry of Christians to the poor and sick throughout history.

Most of the people and events mentioned in both the Old and New Testaments of the Bible can be verified through current archaeological and secular historical sources. In fact, the rise and fall of nations, which were predicted by the prophets of God many centuries in advance of their actual occurrence, all happened with astonishing historical accuracy, which cannot be denied.[1]

Then, there are the 351 Old Testament prophecies concerning the first advent and life of Jesus Christ, with corresponding fulfillment in the New Testament, which would simply be impossible for any human to predict without the insight of God. His short thirty-three-year life on this earth had such a profound impact on the whole world that we divided all of human history into BC and AD eras around His life. Who else can make this claim? No one!

[1] Daniel 2:31–45, Daniel 7:1–27, Revelation 13:1–18

Unfortunately, all this evidence is still not enough to convince many people that God really cares personally about them. So, how can we know for sure the Bible is truly God's word, even to those of us living in the twenty-first century? And by extension, how can we know for sure if Heaven is a real place and not an invented myth?

When it comes to trusting the Lord with the things that matter most to you, there are really only three options to center your personal beliefs around, which in turn will motivate your actions.

Option #1: God will save us.
Option #2: Man will save himself.
Option #3: Man will destroy himself.

Let's take a quick comparative look at each of these worldviews and think about their impact on what we believe about Heaven in general and how we respond to God's true character in particular.

Option #1: God will save us.
- Based on evidence provided by current archeology, modern science, secular history, fulfillment of prophecy, and the personal experiences and testimonies of hundreds of millions of God's people down through history and living currently today.
- Offers Jesus Christ as a role model for values and action.
- Applies the stories and promises in the Bible on a personal level.
- Embraces Creationism and all its ramifications.
- Provides the most compelling and sensible understanding of the original struggle between good and evil, how it has played out over history, and what the ultimate resolution will be.

Option #2: Man will save himself.
- Based on faulty opinions, conclusions, and evidence provided by counterfeit church, political, and scientific authorities who mislead those who are not taught how to weigh the evidence and think rationally and independently for themselves.
- Offers the rich and powerful as role models for values and action.
- Portrays the Bible, Jesus Christ, and God as myths.
- Embraces the theory of evolution and all its ramifications.

- Provides no rational explanation for the titanic struggle between good and evil, how it has played out over history, and a discussion about a heavenly future is not even in the picture.
- Popular science-fiction TV shows and movies support this theory by conditioning the mind to think we will ultimately resolve all our problems on earth and then reach out into space to battle other "evil" civilizations and colonize their worlds too.

Option #3: Man will destroy himself.

- Based on a pessimistic view that modern man is destined to destroy himself either through environmental mismanagement, nuclear war, or some other global extinction-level event.
- Offers protesters and demonstrators as role models for action.
- Readily believes conspiracy theories and lies of all kinds.
- Embraces the theory of evolution and all its ramifications, but despairs of man being able to evolve enough to save himself.
- Provides no hope for a long-term future nor any hope of a life after death, which invalidates any discussion of Heaven.

For me, **option #1** provides the most reasonable explanation of the conflict we see (and experience!) each day all around us between the forces of good and evil, right and wrong. Without faith in the story of the great controversy between Christ and Satan, we only have two other choices. We can live our lives under the false hope of man evolving enough to save himself. Or we can live with no real hope for the future at all, which is meaningless at best and suicidal at worst. Yet, God still gives each one of us the choice.

The Bible explicitly says, "Trust in the Lord with all your heart and lean not unto your own understanding. In all your ways, acknowledge Him, and He will direct your paths." (Proverbs 3:5–6)

Without any doubt in my mind, the Lord has repeatedly fulfilled this promise to me. Many hundreds of millions of Christians down through history would be quick to add their own personal testimony of how the Lord has given them guidance, direction, and protection during some of the most pivotal moments in their lives.

But this promise does not mean there will never be any questions about what God does or does not allow to happen in our lives. We all face the tests of faith and the trials of sin, which can be truly heartbreaking and severe. It is during these times, when our anguished prayers don't seem to get any higher than the ceiling in our room, that the most important concept in this book comes into play. And what is this concept? In a single word, TRUST.

We **must** deliberately choose to trust the Lord with our lives, loved ones, finances, and our worldly dreams, talents, and possessions. And we must trust the Lord with ALL the events that happen in our lives, those we understand and *especially those we don't understand*, from the time we accept Him as our Savior, until we take our last breath.[2]

In fact, *only* this level of trust will enable us to face the death of a loved one or our own death with the calm assurance that looks forward to the resurrection at Christ's second coming. And this same kind of mature trust enables us to have the unshakable confidence that we will totally enjoy our eternal life with God and the saved in Heaven and on the New Earth.

---

[2] Psalm 34:18

PART VIII
FINAL THOUGHTS

Epilogue

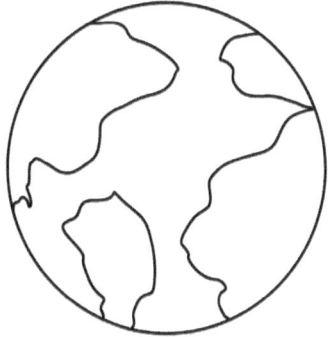

It has been said there will be at least two big surprises for us right away when we get to Heaven—those who are there and those who are not. Some of us will want to know why a particular loved one is not there. Others of us will want some fast answers as to why a particular person actually is there. (Example: The people that Paul persecuted and condemned to death as Saul.) And of course, virtually ALL of us will want answers for the many unexplained events, circumstances, and seemingly unanswered prayers that tested our faith the most during our life on this old sinful world.

Thankfully, we will have plenty of time to get all our questions answered to our complete satisfaction during the one-thousand-year millennium in Heaven.[1] During this time, we will be privileged to look at all the records the heavenly hosts have kept for any and all humans who ever lived on our planet.[2] And we will see precisely why they were mercifully excluded from Heaven by their own words, actions, attitudes, and choices.

Meanwhile, Satan and his demon angels will be chained to the bottomless pit of a totally wreaked planet earth, with no one else alive to

---

[1] Revelation 20:6
[2] Revelation 20:4

tempt.³ They will have this time to contemplate the results of their own choices. But no remorse or shame will be found in them. This will become evident to all the inhabitants of the universe at the end of the millennium.

Now, 1,000 years have passed. The Bible says God will transport the entire holy city, with all the saved inside, through space and land it on what remains of our old earth.⁴ This marks the time for the wicked to be raised to face their final judgment.⁵ The Bible says that Satan and his demons will convince the multitude of the wicked from all ages that they can take the New Jerusalem by force.⁶

We don't know how much time they are allowed to gather, train, and equip their enormous forces. Undoubtedly, they will also have to repair at least some of the wreaked infrastructure of earth to manufacture a variety of modern weapons to arm their forces. Eventually, they get ready to launch their all-out assault by surrounding the City of God. Remember, the New Jerusalem measures about 375 miles long per side. So, think about how many people it would take to totally surround a city of this size! The Bible simply states they are as numberless as the sands of the sea.⁷

Just as they launch the Battle of Armageddon, the wicked are stopped in their tracks and shown in graphic detail when, where, and how they rejected the final pleas of the Holy Spirit.⁸ At the end of this presentation, the Bible says that EVERY knee shall bow and EVERY tongue confess Jesus Christ as Lord of all.⁹ Satan's character and the results of his separation from God have been fully demonstrated to all. God's character and His intentions for fallen humanity have also been fully vindicated before the angels and all beings on unfallen worlds.

---

³ Revelation 20:1–3
⁴ Revelation 21:2
⁵ Revelation 20:5
⁶ Revelation 20:7–8
⁷ Revelation 20:8
⁸ Revelation 20:12–13
⁹ Philippians 2:9–11

At this point, there is no longer any reason whatsoever to tolerate the wicked and their sinful ways. The Bible says fire will come down from God and consume the wicked, just like a piece of wood is consumed when it is thrown into a fire.[10] Of course, their suffering is in proportion to their sinful deeds. Some burn up quickly while others suffer far longer. Satan and his fallen angels suffer the longest, with Satan himself being the last to expire.[11]

During this time, the righteous are safe within the New Jerusalem, which floats on the molten sea of hellfire covering the entire surface of our planet. The Bible says that even the oceans and the atmosphere of earth will be on fire.[12] But only with our eyes will we behold the destruction of the wicked.

While the wicked are being destroyed, the fires of hell will also cleanse the whole earth from every germ, bacteria, and virus, and all pollution, right down to the most microscopic level. Every single man-made object, from the largest buildings to the smallest dwellings, and all of mankind's technical wonders, including the mightiest weapons of mass destruction buried deep underground or sitting at the bottom of the sea, will be reduced to their subatomic particles. When the fires of hell have consumed every single trace of sin from every element on our entire planet and burned out, the end result will be nothing but pure, clean ashes beneath our feet.[13]

Then, we will get to watch something extraordinarily marvelous, which I am looking forward to with great anticipation. We will get to watch God re-create the entire surface of our planet into what it used to be before sin entered the picture.[14] This is why the Bible calls it the New Earth.[15]

---

[10] Revelation 20:9–10
[11] Ezekiel 28:18, Malachi 4:1
[12] 2 Peter 3:10–12
[13] Malachi 4:3
[14] 2 Peter 3:13
[15] Revelation 21:1

Approximately seventy-one percent of the total surface area of our current earth is uninhabitable by humans due to being covered with vast oceans of water.[16] Of the remaining twenty-nine percent of total surface area, which is land, a substantial percentage is either frozen tundra or covered with large deserts. In fact, only a small percentage of our planet's total surface area is inhabited by the current human population of over 7.8 billion people.[17]

But this will not be the case on the New Earth. Some believe the reverse ratio of land to sea from what we currently have prevailed before Noah's flood. This belief is based on current geological evidence, which points to a temperate climate with no polar ice caps and no deserts at all as being in existence before the flood. So, it stands to reason that the New Earth will be created in the same way.

So, with most of the oceans gone, and all the land area restored to a temperate climate, the end result would be a simply enormous reserve of land. Each saved person from all of human history could have many, many square acres of land comprising everything from mountains, forests, and plains, to lakes, rivers, and even beach-front property on the remaining inland seas. Yes, there will be plenty of room for the saved to enjoy country mansions, ranches, farms, mountain villas, and seaside resorts of all descriptions with their family and friends for eternal living at its very finest.

But this won't be our only dwelling place. We will still have our own mansions in the capital city of the New Earth, which is the New Jerusalem. This is where we will live first, for 1,000 years, while it is located in Heaven.[18] It is also where we will return to from one Sabbath to another to worship God in a corporate assembly after He restores both mankind and our planet to what it was originally intended it to be.[19]

To conclude this book, I'd like to share the very best description

---

[16] https://www.usbr.gov/mp/arwec/water-facts-ww-water-sup.html
[17] https://www.theworldcounts.com/
[18] Revelation 20:6
[19] Isaiah 66:23

I have ever read on the subject of how things will be for us after the entire war between Christ and Satan is completely over and done with. Here it is:

> *One pulse of harmony and gladness beats through the vast creation. From Him who created all, flow life and light and gladness throughout the realms of illimitable space. From the minutest atom to the greatest world, all things animate and inanimate, in their unshadowed beauty and perfect joy, declare that God is love.*[20]

My prayer for all of us who must live in the here and now is this: May God grant us the grace to accept the things we cannot change, **the courage to change the things we can**, and the wisdom to know the difference. Amen.

All praise, majesty, power, and glory be to God for ever and ever!

---

[20] White, E. G. (1911) *The Great Controversy.* Mountain View, CA: Pacific Press Publishing Association, p 678

Author's Postscript

†

*My beloved wife,
Angebie Talaroc Drake
1974–2021*

†

I began the manuscript for this book about five years ago. Since that time, I have researched, written, and revised each section many times over. My target audience was single teenagers and adults who had recently lost a spouse. I never imagined that God would call upon me to join the latter group during the final finishing phase of this book.

I can now personally testify that the last three paragraphs of the section entitled "The Most Important Thing" are absolutely essential to our Christian walk at times like this. In fact, we all must choose to TRUST the Lord with all our pain, heartache, and unanswered questions no matter what our circumstances may be.

Fortunately, we have the blessed hope of seeing our loved ones on resurrection morning, never more to be separated again.[1] The Bible speaks of death like a split-second of sleep, from which we either wake up at the resurrection of the saved, or at the resurrection of the judged.[2] God gives each one of us the power of choice in this great controversy between good and evil.

If we choose to live for Him, He makes us this absolute promise

---

[1] Isaiah 65:17, 1 Corinthians 13:12–13, Revelation 21:4
[2] Ecclesiastes 9:5–6, 1 Thessalonians 4:13–17, John 5:28–29, Revelation 20:5

found in Revelation 21:4: "He will wipe every tear from their eyes, and there will be no more death or sorrow or crying or pain. All these things are gone forever." (NLT)

Come soon, Lord Jesus. Amen.

Your Feedback Matters

Rainbow City was written for the glory of God. Its goal was to inspire a more meaningful vision of the places Holy Scripture describes as Heaven and the New Earth. I want to know if it met its goal. If you were encouraged by this book, I would love to hear all about it.

Please leave an honest, personal review online or email your thoughts directly to me at rainbowcity.feedback@gmail.com. And remember to spread the good news about what God is preparing for us by telling your family and friends. Thank you for reading my book!

About the Author

Author Robert E. Drake with his late wife, Angie

Robert E. Drake holds a master's degree from East Tennessee State University and worked for over a decade as a classroom teacher and later, as a technology coordinator. He currently works as an IT systems analyst for Life Care Centers of America.

Before his beloved wife of sixteen years passed away, Robert's passion was spending quality time with her. They were an extremely close couple and could often be seen walking hand in hand in the neighborhood where they lived in Collegedale, Tennessee.

Since Angie was Filipino, they made regular trips overseas to visit family and friends. On these trips, Angie was always asked to sing, and Robert was always asked to teach and preach. They really enjoyed working and ministering together as a close-knit team!

Robert is looking forward to resurrection morning with great anticipation. He plans to spend eternity living, loving, and learning with Angie and giving all the praise, honor, and glory to the One who makes it all possible.

www.ingramcontent.com/pod-product-compliance
Lightning Source LLC
Chambersburg PA
CBHW021427070526
44577CB00001B/100